Following
a
female
Line

Also by Jeanette Stokes

25 Years in the Garden

Hurricane Season
Living Through a Broken Heart

35 Years on the Path

Flying Over Home

Following a female Line

Jeanette Stokes

Jeanette Stokes

Words & Spirit
Durham, North Carolina

Following a Female Line

Designed by Designing Solutions, LLC
Printed in the United States of America.

ISBN 978-0-9821848-7-5

Library of Congress Control Number: 2015943083

First Edition, 2015
10 9 8 7 6 5 4 3 2 1

Copies of this book may be ordered from:
Words & Spirit
1202 Watts Street
Durham, NC 27701
wordsandspirit@aol.com

For Jane, May, and Mary Jeanette

"They went west. I came back."

— Jeanette Stokes

Contents

Women in My Family

One
Creek
Files Valley, Texas, 1950s

On a hot July afternoon, I took off my socks and Keds and set them on the uneven ground beside the little creek. I was a finicky six-year-old and did not like to get dirty, but I enjoyed putting my feet in that creek, even in the squishy mud. The scrubby oak trees that grow in north central Texas were taller along the creek and formed a gentle roof overhead, making it the coolest spot for miles around.

MamaMay pointed up the bank on the other side of the creek as she described the grand parties she had attended sixty years before at Uncle Lee's house, a big, boxy two-story wooden structure across the creek from her childhood home. The abandoned house was still standing, but its bare clapboard siding and broken windows made it look haunted rather than festive. I was more interested in the cool water tickling my toes than stories of elegant soirées my grandmother remembered from her childhood. Still, I listened with one ear, storing the tales just in case they turned out to be important.

Every time my grandmother and I drove the dozen miles from her house in Grandview (population 1,000) out to the creek in Files Valley, she would tell me about the great clan of which I was a part. All of our relatives had moved into nearby towns decades before, but since she was born in the valley and called May Files, my grandmother loved showing me her birthplace. Files Valley is a mild depression in the earth created by the little creek to which five generations of our family had turned for water or pleasure.

That day at the creek, MamaMay knew she didn't have much time. Though I was her oldest grandchild, I lived several hundred miles away. She only had me for a few weeks in the summer and at

Christmas, and she was working against the inevitability of aging, hers and mine. Though the women of her family lived a long time, I'd be a teenager in no time at all. Having raised three children of her own, she must have known she'd lose my attention soon enough. She couldn't trust the family legacy to be transmitted by her daughter, my mother, who had married a doctor and gone off to the bright lights of a big city in God-forsaken Oklahoma. The doctor was a Baptist, with English roots, and would be of no use at all in these matters.

My grandmother's mission was to hook me as closely as possible to the Presbyterian Church, the Files family, and the valley in which we stood. I thought we took idle trips to a cooling spring in the dead of summer, but she had a larger plan. I remember studying the Children's Catechism beside her, going to church with her, visiting her older sisters in nearby Itasca, and driving through the almost flat open landscape out to the valley. The actual words she said to me have moved into my unconscious, beyond hearing, but they must be there, inside, where they took hold and helped to form me.

On that hot summer afternoon, my tiny feet planted in the rocks and mud of the Files Valley Creek, I was totally unaware that my grandmother was shaping my future.

* * *

It would be nearly forty years before I noticed how successful she had been in her plan. She was long dead, and I was a Presbyterian clergywoman before I realized that my grandmother had made me a minister, and she didn't even know it was an option.

This revelation came when I attended my first (and only) Texas family reunion in 1994. It was a gathering of MamaMay's relatives; and though my grandmother was long dead, I was determined to go. I was not going to miss a chance to be with seventy-five of my closest relatives. I had the feeling that I would learn something about myself that I needed to know.

"Your daughter is going to have a pointy chin," I said to the young man holding the baby at the reunion. He looked at me as though he could have lived his whole life quite happily without ever hearing that. He had recently married into the family and had no idea what I was talking about, so I told him. "We all have them," I said as I turned my head sideways and pointed to my chin. I don't think he understood. I don't think pointy chins are a big deal to people who aren't Scots-Irish.

I kept mentioning chins until a cousin from Austin finally responded. "Of course," she said. "We all have pointy chins, deep-set eyes, and high foreheads." I knew I was not making it up. Finally someone agreed! I could give it up, about the chins. But there was more.

Just before lunch, my Uncle Oscar Lee approached me and asked me to return thanks. As an ordained minster, I did get asked to pray on the spot sometimes. But my mind went blank, and I couldn't think of what to say. Food, thank God for the food. I began, "Let us pray," and then I left my body. I heard myself say, "Gracious God, we are grateful that you have brought us to this day. We are grateful for this family, for the Presbyterian General Assembly taking place this weekend, and for the food we are about to receive. Let it nourish our bodies so that we might go forth from this place and show forth the values that have been taught to us by your son Jesus Christ, by the Presbyterian Church, and by the Files Family. Amen."

What was I thinking? Thanking God for the meal, the Presbyterians, and the family! The food was dead animals, for God's sake! I had been furious at the Presbyterian Church (USA) for years for the way they dealt with gay men and lesbians. I was a Democrat, a feminist, and a vegetarian in the middle of a rich Texas Republican meat-producing family.

I wanted the floor to open up and swallow me. Instead I ate my lunch, or rather picked the sliced meat out of my sandwich while my first husband made attempts at conversations with the other "married-ins." I don't think anyone noticed my discomfort.

What I discovered in that mortifying moment was that I was one of them. I thought I had lived my own life and made my own choices, but all of a sudden, it felt like my being a Presbyterian minister had been predestined. While I sometimes mocked my conservative Texas relatives, I had hung onto that family for a huge part of my identity. When I was honest, I had to admit that it was deeply important to me that I came from somewhere and that I knew who my people were.

My grandmother did her job well. She gave me a passionate connection to her family, to the Presbyterian church, and to Texas just as surely as she gave me her pointy Scots-Irish chin. I know what to do with my chin: hold it down when I'm having my picture taken. The attachment to the church still sometimes gives me fits. And I have no idea what I'm going to do with the small bits of Texas land that will come to me when my mother dies.

Some time after the reunion, I began exploring my grandmother's family. Who were these people, and how had they managed to instill in me an almost irrational attachment to family lands in Texas, a feeling that I was one of them, no matter how infrequently I saw them, and enough love for the Presbyterian Church that I'd eventually be ordained as one of its ministers?

Two
Motherline

On Mother's Day, 2005, I called my eighty-three-year-old mother from the parking lot of a beach house where I was spending the week. As we talked, I walked through the maritime forest and out to a pavilion on the beach. She said she was doing fine, which was notable, given her age. It was about 10:30 a.m. my time, and my stepfather had just left for church. Mother was getting dressed so they could go to lunch at the country club when he returned. She had gone to church every Sunday of her life for the first sixty-some years until she wore out on a succession of not very interesting Presbyterian ministers at her neighborhood church and flat-out quit. I could always find her at home between eleven and twelve o'clock on Sunday mornings.

I asked her a few questions about some of our ancestors, since that's what I had been writing about all week. She answered patiently and then mentioned that she had been looking through an old box of pictures and albums and had come across my baby book. The book included a place to record parents, grandparents, and great-grandparents. She said she could tell that her father had filled in the spaces for himself, my grandmother, and his parents. Mother recognized the illegible way he wrote *Wilkirson* and noted, "If you didn't know what it said, you wouldn't have been able to tell by the way he wrote it." But I knew what she had taught me, that their *Wilkirson* was spelled with a second "i" instead of an "e."

Mother said she noticed there was a blank space in the baby book where someone should have written Jane Simpson, her mother's mother. That's when she wondered aloud about what had ever happened to Jane Simpson's people. She said she had asked her younger brother, who still lived in the small Texas town where they were raised, but he didn't seem to know.

I spent the next few years trying to figure out what happened to "Jane Simpson's people." At some points, I was almost obsessed, staying awake into the wee hours of the morning trying to figure out which Mary Moore had married John Simpson and was Jane Simpson's grandmother. When answers surfaced from family records, history books, random discoveries on the Internet, emails from relatives, or Ancestry.com, I'd get excited and call my mother to say, "I found another one of your relatives!"

* * *

My mother grew up in Grandview, Texas, a town of about 1,000 people. She was born on May 25, 1922, in nearby Waxahachi, where there was a hospital. If I mention her birthday, Mother reminds me that an unusual amount of rain meant that to get to the hospital, her mother had to be ferried across a creek in a boat. My grandparents named their only daughter Mary Jeanette and took her home to their two-bedroom cottage on the main north-south street in Grandview.

I grew up in Tulsa, Oklahoma, but spent a lot of time in Grandview with my maternal grandmother, MamaMay, the one who took me wading in Files Valley Creek. We had a comfortable relationship. I was her first grandchild, and she was my favorite grandmother. Always happy to see me, she made it easy for me to adore her.

Mother and I made the six-hour car trip from Tulsa to Grandview several times a year. Well south of the Red River, with Oklahoma far behind us, I'd still be asking, "Are we in Texas yet?" In my mind, Texas encompassed the tiny towns of Grandview and Itasca, "the valley" near Itasca, and the wide-open farm and ranch lands that spread out in every direction around them. I had no interest in the rest of the state. My people were farmers and cattle ranchers. I thought they owned Texas and had been there since time began, which must have been just a few years before my grandmother was born.

I spent several weeks in Grandview most summers until I was twelve, when summer camp with my best friend Sally trumped hanging out with my grandmother. But when I was young, Mother would pack me up with toys and art projects and take me to her mother's, where I became a resident of another world. In Texas, we had dinner in the middle of the day, black women cooked and ironed in the kitchen, and my grandmother was forever driving to Itasca to see about her sisters, while my male relatives counted cows in pastures or sold cars "down at the place" in the middle of town.

I'm sure my mother wanted me to have a relationship with her extended family, but I doubt she understood how much cultural transmission and indoctrination she was facilitating. Perhaps unknowingly, she left it to MamaMay to tell me who I was, or at least my grandmother's version of who I was. By taking me to see the family homestead, telling me stories, and dipping my feet in the creek, my grandmother baptized me into her "religion," which consisted of a fierce devotion to the Presbyterian Church, to her Scots-Irish family, and to the land they owned.

As I sat in my favorite window at the beach cottage in 2005, I stared out at the ocean, the same ocean my ancestors crossed when they came from the British Isles, some of them as many as 250 years ago. I had a strong suspicion that many of the values and commitments those hardy people brought with them were still alive in me. While I might describe myself as a progressive Democrat and a feminist, I was also a Presbyterian minister. I was fascinated by Jane Simpson's people. I wanted to know more about who they were and how they had bound me so closely to their faith, their family, and their land.

* * *

Jane Simpson (my mother's mother's mother) was born in North Carolina in 1846 just east of the modern city of Charlotte. I had not lived in North Carolina long before I decided I was probably related to all the Simpsons in the state. And there are plenty of them.

I grew up in Oklahoma but found my way back to North Carolina after college. Here's how that went.

My Texas mother and Georgia father met in Dallas in 1943 during "the war" (World War II). Mother was just out of college and working as a social worker, and Daddy was finishing a medical residency in obstetrics and gynecology at Parkland Hospital. After they married, in 1944, Daddy was recruited to Tulsa, a town that was expanding with the oil industry. So, I was born and grew up in the "Oil Capital of the World," as Tulsa was known until Houston claimed the title when the big oil companies began moving there in the 1970s.

When it was time to choose a college, I selected Smith College in Northampton, Massachusetts. Having visited the campus only once, on a warm day in April, I would later claim I was tricked by the weather. I enjoyed my college experience, but I did not like the brusqueness of New Englanders or the cold damp winters, which lasted from mid-October to mid-April.

After graduation, I followed my boyfriend Ed, a native North Carolinian, to the Triangle (Raleigh/Durham/Chapel Hill). While he attended the law school at the University of North Carolina, I lived with a Smith friend in Durham and soon enrolled in the divinity school at Duke.

Mother may have reminded me that Jane Simpson was born in my new state, or she may have waited until I remarked on how many women looked like my grandmother. At Ed's family's Presbyterian church in Greensboro, I was struck by how many of the older women looked like MamaMay and her sisters, with the high foreheads, deep-set eyes, and strong chins so characteristic of the Scots-Irish.

I felt at home in North Carolina almost immediately, though it took me several years to realize that by falling in love with a North Carolina man and following him south, I had, in a sense, come home.

On visits back to Tulsa, Mother and I often consulted the family history to look up a cousin or read though the brief section about Jane's ancestors, beginning with William and Martha Simpson, who arrived in the Carolinas in 1772. I always wondered why there wasn't more information about our maternal line and concluded the Simpsons had either all died or that none of them ever amounted to anything, for if they had, my grandmother would have told me about them.

It wasn't until the twenty-first century and my umpty-umpth visit to Grandview that my favorite uncle, Oscar Lee, pointed out the farm just out of town where the Simpsons had lived for a time. I had warmed the passenger seat of a pickup truck and ridden past the spot dozens of times on the way to count cows with my grandfather or my uncle, but no one had ever said a word about that farm. My uncle didn't even seem all that interested in it.

Bewildered at never having been told where the Simpsons lived, I wondered whether my relatives simply forgot the female lines of our family or whether there was something more to the story. I had been doing some research on Jane's siblings, was having trouble finding much information about them, and began to suspect that something more than the usual patriarchal bias was getting in the way.

I knew that Jane was born in North Carolina in 1846, that her family had migrated to Arkansas in the 1850s and then down into Texas in the 1860s. I knew Jane's mother died in Arkansas and her father remarried, but I was having a hard time finding details on her sisters and brothers. She had ten or twelve of them. My mother knew nothing about them, and all my uncle remembered was that some of them had lived "over in Blooming Grove." With my grandmother's interest in her relatives, I wondered why she'd never mentioned these people. She had helped produce the family history on her father's people, the Files family. Her Simpson grandparents died before she was born, but surely she would have known something about Simpson aunts, uncles, or cousins?

I was curious about the breaks in the story. What killed Jane Simpson's mother? What happened to the brother who disappeared from the records after the Arkansas census in 1860? And what of the sisters I couldn't locate? Did they die or get married and stay behind somewhere? This side of my family had given me an almost irrational attachment to family, faith, and land. I wanted to know who these people were and whether they had been able to hold onto one another as they risked everything in moving west.

Martha Orr Simpson

(1752–1832)

Three
Hunting for My Ancestors
Charlotte, North Carolina

When I first lived in North Carolina, I liked to say that I was related to everyone in the state named Simpson, though I had no real evidence to support my claim. I wondered about a guy in the class ahead of me, Mitch Simpson, but never even pursued the question with him. In random conversations over the next few years, I'd mention that some of my ancestors came from down near Charlotte. The conversations rarely went anywhere until I met Sally Thomas in 1982 at a conference on women and economic justice. Sally was an accountant and active Presbyterian who lived in Charlotte. Perhaps she told me that she was from Arkansas, because for some reason I mentioned that my great-grandmother Jane Simpson was born on Four Mile Creek somewhere near Charlotte and that she moved with her family to Arkansas. However the conversation went, Sally said she was sure she had passed a sign for Four Mile Creek, maybe on a bridge somewhere in the southern part of town. She promised that if I'd come to Charlotte, she'd take me to the library, where I could look through old deeds and records for clues about my ancestors.

A few years later, in 1995, when I took a long break from my job as the director of the Resource Center for Women and Ministry in the South, I took Sally up on her offer. My first husband and I went to Charlotte for something that had to do with his work and stayed with Sally and her husband. The men discussed their enthusiasm for drumming, and then Sally and I spent several hours in the archives at the library. That was almost twenty years ago and the point at which I first waded into the river of paper that promises to contain a family's history.

Sally took me downtown to the Main Branch of the Charlotte Mecklenburg Library. The building's impressive glass and block facade suggested that its contents had to be important. Leaving the rumble of traffic, we walked through a two-story archway, pulled open an enormous glass door, and entered a wide lobby. As I admired the high ceilings and large geometric patterns on the floor, Sally pointed us in the direction of the Carolina Room. Tall arched windows brightened the large room dedicated to North Carolina research, and long tables invited even the novice to spread out papers and books and get to work.

It was my first experience in looking up two-hundred-year-old documents, but with the help of a librarian, I figured out how to use books that indexed wills, deeds, and birth certificates. In one, I located a mention of a deed from James and Margaret Orr to "Will'm" Simpson, filed in October 1787. The property description was simply, "Crooked Cr." Ah, so there was another creek several states away from the one where I waded with MamaMay, another creek that was important to my family's survival.

When I looked for the deed book on microfiche, I found an almost illegible copy of the deed with Margaret and James Orr's signatures or marks.

> This Indenture made the eighth day of September in the year one thousand seven hundred & eighty five between Jas Orr of the county of Mecklenburg & state of No Carolina & Margaret his wife of the one part & William Simpson of the county of Mecklenburg....

There it was—proof that my people had been in North Carolina.

Something shifted in me that day in the Carolina Room. Something changed. I knew that Jane Simpson was born in North Carolina and that her people had owned land in the state. But looking at a legal document, a deed to land in North Carolina, changed everything as much as pulling a piece of candy out of a glass case and putting it in my mouth would. I wanted to disturb the quiet room and yell, "Eureka! I found them." The Simpsons were real people who had lived less than thirty miles from where I sat.

It would be over a decade before I met members of the Simpson clan in Charlotte and walked on land once owned and occupied by my ancestors, but I had stepped into the river of history. Though

I wasn't sure exactly where the Simpson's property had been, I found Crooked Creek and Four Mile Creek on a map—long creeks running roughly east-west though modern Mecklenburg and Union Counties.

Once I knew where they lived, I wanted to know more about who the Simpsons were and how they came to live in North Carolina in the first place. And if they had come to love North Carolina as much as I had, why had they left it to move west?

Four
Scots-Irish

"What am I?" I would ask my mother when I was young. "Scots-Irish and English," she'd reply. I thought that meant some of my ancestors came from Scotland, some from Ireland, and some from England. It was probably what my mother thought, and while it's mostly true, it's more complicated than that.

I tried calling myself *Scots-Irish* when I was visiting Scotland in the mid-1970s, but local people had no idea what I was talking about. To them, people in Scotland were Scots and people in Ireland were Irish (whether Protestant or Catholic). They had no idea what something *Scots-Irish* might be.

A decade later, Shirley Abbott's *Womenfolks: Growing Up Down South* explained what I am. I'm Scots-Irish and English. *Scots-Irish* refers to Irish Protestants (Presbyterians), who immigrated to the United States by the thousands in the 1700s to escape mistreatment by the English. The term did not come into use, however, until the influx of Irish Catholics in the 1800s when the Protestant Irish wanted to distinguish themselves from the Catholic newcomers. The Protestants had been in America long enough to move up in society and didn't want to be confused with the new lower-class immigrants from the same country. *Scots-Irish* is a term based on prejudice. It was part of the terrible discrimination against Irish Catholics that produced want ads in US cities that read, "NINA," *No Irish Need Apply.*

Having grown up with an Irish Catholic President, John F. Kennedy, I had a hard time grasping this particular form of discrimination, but the late-twentieth-century conflicts in Northern Ireland help me believe it was fierce and existed on both sides of the Atlantic.

The modern conflicts between Protestants and Catholics have roots that are four or five hundred years old. I like to say that these conflicts are the fault of our ancestors, possibly yours and certainly mine.

As an American, I find the history of the English monarchs hard to remember. What I am able to hang onto is the fact that in the 1500s and 1600s, the English crown was always switching back and forth between Protestants and Catholics, and that if you were on the wrong team when the switch happened, you might lose your job, your country, or your life.

The English reformation began in 1533 when Henry VIII of England wanted a divorce and breaking ties with the Pope was the only way to get it. Henry didn't actually object to being Catholic, he just wanted to get a divorce and marry Anne Boleyn. Unable to wrangle a papal annulment for his twenty-four-year marriage to Catherine of Aragon, Henry married Anne anyway in 1533, effectively making himself a Protestant.

I had always assumed that the Presbyterians (in Scotland and Ireland) were better off when the English had a Protestant monarch. I have come to understand that it didn't matter whether the crown was Protestant or Catholic; the English were always threatening the Presbyterians with something.

The Scots and the Irish are woven together by geography, history, and ethnicity and divided by religion, politics, and class. Genetically, there's no difference between a Scottish and an Irish person (but don't try to tell them that).[1] Though they developed distinct national identities, even after that, they were as mixed together as sand sloshing around in a bucket. The sloshing was caused, in part, by the way the Scots moved around, movement that was motivated by the English crown and by a never ending search for good land.

In fact, my Scottish ancestors may have started out in Ireland, as a tribe called Scotia, and crossed the sea. A mere thirteen miles of water separate Northern Ireland from a Scottish peninsula that sticks out west of Glasgow. Any fool with a boat could sail across, or get blown across by accident. Anyway, my ancestors in Scotland would have thought of themselves as thoroughly Scottish by the early 1600s when the English started moving them around.

In the 1600s, when the English crown wanted to get a stronger foothold in Ireland, groups of Anglicans and Presbyterians were relocated to Ulster (in Northern Ireland). The "Plantation of Ulster" began in 1610. Many Scots took the crown up on the offer of land in Ireland, and by 1641, there were a million and a half Protestant Scots in Ireland. None too pleased with the intruders, the Irish rose up that same year and killed something like ten thousand Protestants. A few years later, Oliver Cromwell retaliated by massacring Catholics. It wasn't what you'd call a good situation for anyone.

The English had simply stolen land from the native Irish and given it to English nobles and Scottish settlers, leaving the native Irish Catholics to live and work as serfs, nearly as slaves, on their own land. That plan should sound familiar because it is almost exactly like the system their descendants, the descendants of both the English and the Scots-Irish, used when they got to America. I guess that conquering people have used it all over the globe, but the British perfected it.

There were three distinct groups in Ulster in the 1700s. English Anglicans owned the land, set the rents, and controlled the government; Scottish Presbyterians rented land; and displaced Irish Catholics provided cheap labor. The Scots were treated as second-class citizens under English control. Marriages performed by Presbyterian clergy were not considered legal by the Church of England, even though the Irish Presbyterians were forced to support the English Church with their tithes. Perhaps worst of all, English nobles owned the land the Presbyterians farmed.

So, a hundred years after the Scots migrated to Ireland, many of their descendants were ready to move on. In the early 1700s, new English laws discriminated against all non-Anglicans (including Catholics and Presbyterians). Also, thousands of Ulster land leases came due in 1717 and 1718, rents were raised, and the Scots (who now simply thought of themselves as Irish) began leaving Ireland for North America. They began streaming across the ocean by the thousands, and then by the tens of thousands, in search of religious freedom, land, and better economic opportunities. As many as 450,000 people left between 1717 and 1770. Having suffered under English rule for generations, the last thing the immigrants wanted was to live in heavily English regions such as New England and Virginia, so they tended to congregate in Pennsylvania, Appalachia, the Carolinas, and Eastern Canada.

Between 1717 and the Revolutionary war, a million people came to the new world from Ulster. Sometimes whole congregations made the move together. Those coming early in the century sailed to Philadelphia, while later in the century the port of Charleston was the most common destination.

When my ancestors, William and Martha Simpson, left Ireland for America in 1772, they certainly thought of themselves as Irish. They were latecomers in the Scots-Irish migration to the new land, but not too late for a land grant.

Five
Martha & William
1772

William and Martha Simpson were the first of my Simpson ancestors to migrate to North America. For decades I knew almost nothing about them. They were names in a list of ancestors in the family history my grandmother helped to publish. *The History of the Files Family* is mostly about the Files (my grandmother's father's people), but it includes one newspaper article about the descendants of William Simpson. Originally published in 1911 in *The Waxhaw Enterprise*, the article lists all of William and Martha's known descendants. It begins with a clue to who these people were.

> Some time prior to the Revolution there lived in the north of Ireland a youth named William Simpson, whose heart was imbued with the love of liberty and the spirit of adventure. He loved, became engaged to and married a girl named Martha Orr, and with his young wife came to America. In the year 1773 he settled on Four Mile Creek, in Mecklenburg County, and built him a little home. His soul soon became fired with the spirit of the Revolution and when the war came he enlisted anxiously and fought bravely until the conflict terminated in its glorious conclusion. This William Simpson was the progenitor of the entire Simpson family in Union (County, North Carolina).[2]

That phrase, "progenitor of the entire Simpson family," was the first clue that I might actually be related to lots of people in North Carolina. When I started looking for more information about the Simpsons, I was amazed at how much information I was able to discover about them. The trip to the Charlotte library I've already mentioned was a big step. After that, thanks to online resources, I found William Simpson's name on a passenger list of the *James and Mary*, a ship that sailed from the port of Larne on the east coast of Northern Ireland to Charleston, South Carolina, in 1772.

In reading about the ship and the voyage, I came across the most startling fact. William and Martha didn't come alone, or even with a few friends or family. They came to America in an organized group of nearly one thousand people. The *James and Mary* was one of five ships that transported this crowd in the fall of 1772. Their Presbyterian minister and leader, Rev. William Martin, organized 467 families to set out for the Promised Land together.

I could hardly believe it: nearly a thousand men, women, and children, on five ships. I couldn't imagine organizing and moving that many people such a long time ago. Pictures of refugees with bundles of clothes and ragged children arriving at Ellis Island came to mind, only that was more than a century later. My disbelief aside, discovering my relatives among this enormous group was a great stroke of luck. Because there were so many of them, they are fairly well documented.

It was hard to imagine why all those people wanted to risk their lives on a perilous sea crossing, leave behind family and the only homeland they had ever known, and move to a strange new place; but apparently they did.

Perhaps it was the combination of hardships at home and a charismatic leader with a vision of a better place that inspired hundreds of people to leave Ireland all at once. Even so, it would take tremendous organizing and inspiring to pull off such an undertaking. The Reverend William Martin was just the man for the job, a preacher who must have been as evangelical about his faith as he was about moving to the American colonies. When he received a call to preach in Upper South Carolina in 1772, Martin was ready to go and to take most of his followers with him.

Born in 1729 near Ballykelly in County Londonderry (Northern Ireland), Martin was educated at the University of Glasgow in Scotland. He was licensed to preach by the Reformed (Covenanter) Presbyterian Church at The Vow, County Antrim.

The term *Covenanter* has a long history in the 1600s and 1700s, which includes the ever-changing relationship among the English crown, the English parliament, and the official government of Scotland. Covenanter Presbyterians objected to their government's concessions to the English Crown.

Covenanters were Presbyterians in the lowlands of Scotland who were devoted to the Presbyterian form of government and who signed a covenant saying they would never swear allegiance to any king except Jesus, certainly not the cursed King of England. They were very conservative Presbyterians who were often at odds with the Church of Scotland, which was constantly making concessions to the English crown. In Scotland, the Covenanters refused to worship in the established (Anglican) churches and preferred to defy the authorities, risk their lives, and gather on the moors. They were such purists that they once lost a battle against the English, because just before the fighting, they purged their ranks of all but "true believers" and drastically reduced their forces. (I recognize this stubborn trait in my relatives and in myself.)

This helps to explain why modern Presbyterians get so upset if anyone suggests they merge with a Protestant denomination that has bishops. Our forebears in Scotland and Ireland risked their lives to worship as they chose, fought battles to protect their form of church government, and fled their homeland in order to avoid being part of a church that had bishops and a royal "head of the church."

The Covenanters spread to Northern Ireland in the early 1700s, and the Reformed Presbytery consolidated in Ulster as early as 1743; but it was not until Rev. Martin's ordination in 1757 that they had a steady missionary preacher. You can find a marker commemorating the event at a beautiful site on the River Bann between Ballymoney and Kilrea, County Antrim.

As the first Covenanter Presbyterian minister ordained in counties Down and Antrim, Martin was active in attempts to recruit or ordain other Covenanter ministers. Still, he was, for most of his time there, the only one working in the area. By 1760, he was living at Kellswater and preaching on a regular circuit at Cullybackey, Leymore, Cloughmills, Dervock, and Londonderry and continuing at The Vow. While it was satisfying work and his flock was large, he was under constant threat of persecution.

By moving, his followers had a chance to escape religious oppression and the economic hardships of high rents for farmers and a depressed linen trade for those who worked in factories. South Carolina offered land grants to settlers who promised to improve the land. All that stood in their way was sailing off the edge of their known world.

In 1772, when Rev. Martin organized his parish to leave Ireland for America, my ancestors William and Martha Simpson were among his flock.

Six
Coming to America
South Carolina

While my Presbyterian ancestors were preparing to leave Ireland, the Presbyterians in Upper South Carolina were having their own theopolitical struggles. By 1770, there were already a lot of Presbyterians in Upper South Carolina, all attracted by the promise of land.

When I say a lot of Presbyterians, I don't just mean there were a lot of individual Presbyterians; I mean lots of different kinds of Presbyterians. There were five or six different kinds of Presbyterians in Upper South Carolina, many of them Covenanters, but there were also Associates, Burghers, Anti-Burghers, Seceders, and more.[3] While I don't understand all the differences, the important thing is that they didn't always get along with one another. Some were descended from Scots who had left Scotland for America generations before and landed in the Northeast. Subsequent generations lived in Pennsylvania, migrated to Virginia and North Carolina, and then moved on to South Carolina. Other Presbyterians in Upper South Carolina were newer arrivals from Ireland. There were so many different kinds of Presbyterians with different histories flowing into the area that they didn't always get along.

It seems relevant at this point to mention that we Presbyterians are famous for our squabbles. (The Hatfields and McCoys were our people.) Our ancestors fought the English for five hundred years, first in Scotland and then in Ireland. They were ferocious fighters for American freedom in the Revolutionary War and then battled with equal zeal to deny African Americans freedom in the Civil War. We have ongoing arguments within our various Presbyterian denominations; disagreements over changes to our form of government have been just as fierce as others over the ordination of people of varying sexual orientations. In the midst of these disagreements, constant reminders that we value "the peace and unity" within the church seem to keep us from name-calling and personal attacks. Like families, we may criticize one another but are mightily offended if anyone from the outside disparages our own.

The various groups of upcountry Presbyterians managed to cooperate long enough to build a church, which they called Catholic Presbyterian Church, and to issue a call for a minister in 1770. Yes, it was called Catholic Presbyterian. Today, we associate *catholic* with the Roman Catholic Church, but *catholic* simply means *universal*. The church's name indicated that several different kinds of Presbyterians were using the building. If you hunt for it on a map today, you can find "Catholic Church Road." Any visitor passing the road would assume it led to, or had once led to, a Roman Catholic church, but they'd be wrong.

In 1770, there were not enough Presbyterian ministers of any description to serve the growing number of Presbyterians in Upper South Carolina. One minister, Rev. William Richardson, pastor of the Waxhaw Presbyterian Church (south of Charlotte, just over the line into South Carolina), traveled to Catholic to preach when he could. But Richardson was given to bouts of depression,[4] may have been increasingly unwell, and died (possibly by his own hand) in 1771. Because of this or for some other reasons, the Covenanters wrote to Northern Ireland in 1770 and asked for a minister. Rev. William Martin answered the call and began to organize many in his parish to accompany him to America.[5]

* * *

William and Martha Orr Simpson must have been about twenty years old when they left for America. It was a costly and difficult journey for anyone, and especially for a young couple traveling with three small children—a two-year-old, a toddler, and a babe in arms. When I figured all this out, I felt so proud of them for embarking on such an adventure.

I wonder what it would have been like to plan to take one's young family so far from home. There must have been many long conversations with family and friends and tearful goodbyes to people they would likely never see again. And what of those left behind? Did they ever expect to see their young adventurers again?

Perhaps Martha Simpson visited her grandmother's grave before leaving. Would it have been located in a churchyard or on a rented farm? Could it have been in view of a creek that emptied into Ballymoney River? If Martha was able to write, she might have recorded it this way.

> The last time I visited Grandmother's grave in Ballymoney, I picked up a small stone. She was such an angel to me; she loved me best, her youngest grandchild. She died when I was eight, but since I bore her name, I felt I had her with me even after she had gone home to be with Jesus. So, I picked up a stone, a small round grey-brown piece of home, not knowing if I'd ever see that place again. And then when we got to Larne on the coast, to the big noisy port, I picked up a seashell. Later, when I showed it to one of the crew, he said it was only half a shell, half of a scallop shell, the other half and the creature that would have lived inside were lost to the sea. In years to come, I may feel like only half of myself, living so far from home.

* * *

I have tried to imagine how the small Simpson family might have traveled the thirty miles from Balleymoney to Larne on the coast. They could have walked, but I hope that the three children and their meager belongings inspired someone to give them a ride in a cart.

They boarded the *James and Mary* at Larne on August 25, 1772. The ship was a type known as a snow, a common two-masted vessel with square sails. For seven weeks, they sailed across the cold Atlantic, arriving in Charles Town Harbor on October 18, only to be refused permission to enter the city. An outbreak of smallpox aboard the *James and Mary*, which had taken the lives of five children, so concerned officials that the survivors were quarantined for seven weeks.[6]

Smallpox was considered so dangerous that no one who had been around it was allowed near the residents of Charles Town. The passengers were allowed to move around between the ship and "the sick house." Martha Simpson might have remembered the harrowing crossing and long confinement this way.

> Not much survived the journey. We carried so little. Managing the three children was hard enough, but I shouldn't complain. We arrived alive. We survived the seven-week crossing and seven more weeks quarantined in Charles Town Harbor. Anything I worried about having with me when we left Ballymoney was used up, worn out, or practically ruined after seven weeks on that wooden sailing vessel and seven more in confinement. Thank God the officials allowed us to get off on the island and allowed us some vegetables, meat, and ale after they figured out there had been smallpox onboard. We were down to the last of the hard dry salted meat by then.

As cramped and dirty as their conditions might have been, I dare say, the white people on the *James and Mary* had more food and fresh air than the Africans who were suffering their own quarantine in holding pens nearby.

CHARLES TOWN HARBOR

The Ashely and Cooper rivers flow around the city of Charleston, mingle their waters in Charleston Harbor, and flow out to the sea between two barrier islands, Sullivan's Island to the north and Morris Island to the south. Sailors, who avoided the shallow shoals and made it through the cut, found themselves in a generous, well-protected harbor. Nearly four miles across, it is no wonder that Charleston Harbor was the busiest Colonial port in the South. Sullivan's Island was named for Captain Florence O'Sullivan, an Irish soldier of fortune, who was on the first British colonizing expedition to the Carolinas in 1670. In the thirteen years he spent on the island before his death in 1683, O'Sullivan served, for a time, as surveyor-general and became a planter of some notoriety. In 1674, O'Sullivan was given the task of placing a "Great Gun" at the mouth of the harbor to protect the new colony developing at Charles Town. Sullivan's Island was later home to Fort Moultrie, which figured prominently in a Revolutionary War battle against the British Navy.[7]

As the colony grew, the people of Charles Town became concerned about their health, and Sullivan's island was designated as the site for quarantine. Sick people were sent to the "pest house" on Sullivan's Island to keep them away from those who were healthy. Whites were concerned about diseases and plagues that might be brought by immigrants, particularly slaves from Africa or the Caribbean. The colonists of Charles Town passed an act in 1744 saying that no ship or vessel could enter the harbor carrying "Negroes" without first putting them on shore at Sullivan's Island.[8] African slaves who had survived the terror, disease, and degradation of the Middle Passage might well catch their death in the hellish, disease-ridden conditions on Sullivan's Island, where they were interned for at least ten days. Forty percent of the slaves who were brought to British North America came in through Charles Town, and for many, Sullivan's Island provided a miserable introduction to their new continent.

There is no way to know what my ancestors or the other Covenanters knew or thought about Africans before they left their home in Balleymoney. Irish merchants were well aware of the wealth that could be made through the growing Atlantic slave trade. While hampered by regulations that required goods to pass through English ports on the way to or from Ireland, the Irish still made economic gains by selling goods to the slave colonies, such as salted and pickled Irish provisions developed to feed slaves and planters in the colonies.

It is possible that the pilgrims headed for South Carolina were told about slave ships before reaching the New World. But even if not, the presence of slave ships in Charles Town Harbor, disgorging Africans onto the same island where the *James and Mary* was anchored, could not have passed unnoticed. I can only imagine that the indoctrination in North American prejudices began early for my ancestors. In their first weeks in South Carolina, I suspect that my ancestors were taught to fear Africans the way they dreaded disease, drought, and the English.

Once released from quarantine, the male passengers of the *James and Mary* sent a letter back to Ireland to let interested parties know they had arrived safely. The letter went first to the ship owner, James McVickar, a merchant in Larne. McVickar then asked the *Belfast News-Letter* to publish it.[9]

22 December 1772

To the PRINTERS of the BELFAST NEWS-LETTER.

I desire you will insert and continue three times in your Paper, the inclosed Letter, which I received from South Carolina.

Yours,

JAMES M'VICKAR.

Larne, 21st Dec. 1772.

P. S. My Friend in Charlestown advises me, that they have a great Crop of Rice, but want Ships to carry it to Market.

The letter from America details the journey and the gratitude of the passengers.

Charles Town, Oct. 21, 1772.

To Mr. JAMES M'VICKAR, Merchant in Larne.

S I R,

THESE will inform you, that we arrived here all well and in good spirits the 18th instant (five Children excepted who died on the Passage) after a pleasant and agreeable Passage of seven weeks and one day. Pleasant with respect to Weather, and agreeable with regard to the Concord and Harmony that subsisted among us all; And, to confirm what we have heard you assert before we left Ireland, we must say, that we had more than a sufficiency of all kinds of Provision, and good in their kind; And to speak of Captain Workman, as he justly deserves, we must say with the greatest Truth, (and likewise with the greatest Thanks and Gratitude to him) that he treated us all with the greatest Tenderness and Humanity; and seemed even desirous of obliging any one, whom it might be in his Power to serve. If you think proper, we would be desirous you should cause these Things to be inserted in the public News-Letter, being sensible they will afford our Friends and Acquaintances great Satisfaction; and we hope they may be of some Use to you and Captain Workman, if you resolve to trade any more in the Passenger Way. Now, in Confirmation of these Things, we subscribe ourselves as follows:

The letter closes with, "We are, Sir, your Most humble Servants," and is signed by thirty-seven men, Wm. Simpson among them. A brief postscript followed. "P.S. We had Sermon every Sabbath, which was great Satisfaction to us. We omitted to let you know, that the Mate, Mr. Bole, as also the common Hands, behaved with great Care and Benevolence towards us."

The report of the preaching on Sunday amuses me. Here we have all the ingredients that were important to my grandmother's family: the family together on the ship, headed to acquire land in America, and practicing their faith all the way.

UPCOUNTRY

By the time the passengers of the *James and Mary* were released from quarantine, it was December 1772. The city that greeted them was as bustling and modern as any in the colonies. The other four ships associated with Rev. William Martin had all arrived by then, were disease-free, and avoided quarantine. Having reassembled, the male passengers began to petition for their land grants.[10]

The story of one passenger on the *James and Mary* helps me to imagine the Simpson's first weeks and months. Alexander Chesney was only a boy when he crossed the Atlantic with his parents. As an adult he become a Loyalist who aided the British and eventually returned to Ireland, where he wrote a journal of his life. Chesney reports that after the quarantine,

When the crew and passengers were recouvered [*sic*] we landed at Prichard's ship-yard on Town Creek, a few miles above Charles Town from whence the passengers proceeded to country as soon as they could respectively find Waggons [*sic*] destined for that part of the country where they meant to settle.[11]

Rev. Martin's call to preach had come from Presbyterians in Upper South Carolina, but even without that upland invitation, I doubt that my ancestors or their companions would have stopped in the lowcountry. Charleston was a well-established city of British culture, commerce, and religion, none of which appealed to the scruffy, scrappy Irish Protestants who were arriving. And I feel quite sure that the Charlestonians had no interest in living with my relatives. My ancestors wanted land where they could establish small farms that could support a family, open areas where they could hunt, and a place where they could worship God in their particular Presbyterian way. Once they got off the ship, they couldn't get through the land office and headed out of the city fast enough.

The Scots-Irish wound up living at the western edges of the colonies all up and down the East Coast, providing a buffer between the more established areas and the wilds to the west, which were still inhabited by Native Americans. (As a matter of fact, I lost some of my Files ancestors in an Indian raid in what was then western Virginia in the 1750s, but I'll tell you about that a bit later.) The Scots-Irish were people of the borderlands and had been for five hundred years. They lived in lowland Scotland along Hadrian's Wall and battled with the English. Living in harsh open country and fighting the border wars bred a sturdy stubborn stock on the Scottish side and a resentment against the English that never wore off. In Ireland they served as both a wedge and a buffer between the English Anglicans and the native Irish Catholics. They left because they were at odds with both.[12]

Scots-Irish who arrived in Philadelphia in the early 1700s wound up farming in Southern Pennsylvania or in the Shenandoah Valley, where they provided a western guard. From there many drifted south into North Carolina and Upper South Carolina. The ones who arrived later in the century, like the Simpsons, came in through Charleston and quickly populated the southern Appalachians.

The crowd of settlers that included the Simpsons came for the promise of land that would be theirs if they worked it. They thought they would also be provided with tools and supplies as earlier settlers to the colony had been, but they got to South Carolina too late for that part of the deal.

The people who emigrated with Rev. William Martin headed to Upper South Carolina, to what is now Chester County, because that is where Rev. Martin had been called to preach. They had hoped to live close to one another, but they were too late for that as well. So much of the land in Upper South Carolina had already been granted that they had to take whatever they could get.

William Simpson's grant, dated December 11, 1772, gave him 200 acres of land in Craven (now Chester) County, South Carolina, on the waters of the Little River, about twenty miles southwest of Rock Hill, and about forty miles southwest of Charlotte, North Carolina. The head of a family was entitled to 100 acres for himself and 50 for each additional member of the family. William was entitled to 300 acres, though the records suggest he only took 200. With three small children, 200 acres may have been all he and Martha thought they could manage.[13]

Seven
Four Mile Creek
North Carolina

William and Martha Orr Simpson didn't stay in South Carolina long. They turn up in official records again in 1787, when they bought a piece of the land on Crooked Creek in Mecklenburg County, North Carolina. (That's the record I found in the Charlotte library on my first attempt to locate them.) Some family records say they settled on Four Mile Creek in 1773. The details of their move from South Carolina to North Carolina are not available, but I'm happy to have the story from Alexander Chesney to help me imagine the Simpsons' first weeks and months in America.

Alexander Chesney describes moving upcountry in a rented wagon, for which his father paid "one penny per pound Weight."[14] Staying first with one relative and then another, the Chesneys soon "got 100 Acres of land surveyed there, built a cabin and cleared some of the land." When they received a letter from a great-aunt, "who resided Pacholet River about sixty miles higher up in the country," they moved to her location.

I expect William and Martha set up housekeeping on their land in South Carolina, constructed a simple dwelling, and began to "improve" the land. They may have stayed through one planting season before receiving a communication from the Orrs in North Carolina, who I suspect were Martha's relatives. The Orrs probably described their good land and the generous creek on which they lived and offered to sell a portion of it to the newcomers. (I notice that immigrants today move around the United States in a pattern similar to people in the 1700s. They go where they know people.) The Simpsons probably sold their land in South Carolina before they bought land from the Orrs in 1787, but I haven't been able to confirm that from the records.

The Simpsons owned land on Crooked Creek and Four Mile Creek in what was then Mecklenburg County and is now mostly in Union County between Charlotte and Monroe, North Carolina.[15] The closest community today is Indian Trail. Creeks were often named in plot descriptions and served as "addresses" for many early settlers. William and Martha's farm was near "the headwaters of Four Mile Creek."

As I studied a map of the area, I discovered the headwaters of Four Mile Creek and the headwaters of the North Fork of Crooked Creek were only about a mile apart. After plotting their courses, I noticed that their paths to the sea formed opposite sides of a long, irregular oval. From sources close together, the two creeks began by flowing in opposite directions. Four Mile Creek flows west through the southern part of Mecklenburg County, into McAlpine Creek and Sugar Creek in South Carolina, and eventually into the Catawaba River. The Catawba joins the Wateree and then the Santee, which is currently dammed up to form Lake Marion, and eventually empties into the Atlantic just south of Georgetown, South Carolina.

Crooked Creek starts just west of the Mecklenburg/Union County line, near modern-day Matthews, North Carolina. It flows east into Union County, joins the South Fork of Crooked Creek, flows into the Rocky River, which joins the Pee Dee and flows to the Atlantic two miles south of the Santee.

These two creeks, so important to my ancestors, take meandering paths away from one another, travel hundreds of miles, and empty into the ocean just two miles apart. As I gazed at the map, I was struck by the way the paths of the creeks resembled the migration of my Scots-Irish ancestors, the Files and the Simpsons. From Scottish soil they found their separate ways to Ireland and then to the southeast coast of North America. The Files and the Simpsons took different paths west across the Mississippi and wound up just a few miles apart in Texas.

* * *

My ancestor John Files received a land grant in South Carolina in 1766 in the old Granville District (which became the Ninety-Six District and then the Abbeville & Pendleton Districts) in the vicinity of modern Anderson, South Carolina.[16] That's in the far northwestern part of South Carolina close to Georgia. In 1772, William Simpson received a land grant eighty or a hundred miles to the northeast, near what is now Chester, South Carolina. What I'm learning is that the whole northwestern quarter of South Carolina was thick with Presbyterians. The area is the Piedmont, just below the foothills of the Appalachians, and includes the modern cities of Spartanburg, Greenville, Anderson, Clinton, and Chester.

The story of how the Files got to South Carolina starts with yet another creek that bears the family name. This Files Creek was not in Texas. It was in West Virginia.

Eight
Foyles (Files)

The Files, or Foyles as they were once called, were already in the American Colonies when the Simpsons arrived. When my great-grandmother Jane Simpson married Frances Marion Files in 1866, she married into a well-established family in North Central Texas. The Files are well documented as successful landowners, ranchers, and business people. Growing up, I constantly heard references to the Files and how special they were, but never anything about the Simpsons.

In America, the Files first show up in the Augusta County, Virginia records. Robert Foyle acquired land there in 1745 on the "North River of Shenando [*sic*], between McGill's and Wilkins'." Robert Foyle appears in the records as a witness, petitioning the court, being appointed as a juryman, suing someone, and having a road approved for his area. In 1748 Foyle is "exempted from levy, being a cripple and unable to labor," so within three years he was injured in some way. In one place he is referred to as "Doctor Robert Foyle," but I have no other information about that.

Like many of his Scots-Irish brethren before and after him, Robert Foyle was involved in a dispute. Virginia court papers include a record of a suit pursued by Foyle.

> Robert Foyle vs. John Erwin.—Slander. Charged that plaintiff had spoken treasonable words. Robert and Elizabeth, his wife, had resided in New Castle County, Pennsylvania, 8 years before 27th May, 1745. One of the Justices certifies that they were good citizens. Many of the citizens certify that they were a common disturber of the peace, both amongst Clergy and Commonwealth. Verdict for plaintiff. 1 penny.[17]

From that, we learn that Robert and Elizabeth lived in Pennsylvania, home of many Scots-Irish who later moved to Virginia. The content of the slander is not stated in the suit, but it is easy to imagine that a man of Foyle's descent might speak badly of the English crown. His people came to this country to get away from the English and were charged with various forms of sedition up and down the East Coast. Robert was called both a good citizen and a common disturber of the peace. That also goes along with the hard-working, rowdy, contentions nature for which the Scots-Irish were known. Even so, it appears that Robert Foyle won his case.

In 1753 Robert and Elizabeth Foyle ventured further west over the Allegheny Mountains into the unprotected wilderness that would eventually become West Virginia. The brave souls were accompanied by their children and by Elizabeth's brother David Tygert and his family. According to sources I consulted, they were the first white families to attempt to inhabit the wilderness that is present-day West Virginia. (One might also think of them as invaders, but American history books rarely see it that way.) The two families settled on an upper branch of the Monongahela River, near what is now Beverly, West Virginia. The area would come to be knows as the Tygert River Valley. Robert and Elizabeth built a cabin where Files Creek meets the Tygert River, and the Tygert family built a few miles away, also on the river. (Colonists had a habit of naming creeks and streams after the first white people who set up housekeeping nearby.)

It seems likely that Robert and his family worked hard to build a cabin and enjoyed the bounty of the forest, particularly the wild game. When I try to imagine the creek, the river, the mountains, and the forest, as they would have been 250 years ago, I see two things. One is an idyllic land inhabited for generations by Native Americans but not depleted by them. No doubt the settlers noticed carefully tended footpaths or fords across rivers and streams. They probably encountered lightweight temporary wooden structures used by the indigenous people for drying meat and fish or as shelter from the rain. Into this more or less balanced ecological system came my wild and wooly ancestors, who, after all those years of fighting the English, had not developed a reputation of living gently on the earth or with their neighbors.

The other thing I see is the devastation wrought by mountain top removal in West Virginia today. Whatever gash my ancestors cut into the landscape was minimal by comparison, but by their mere presence they were opening the way for commerce and ecological destruction. They brought with them a Protestant ethic that suggested that nature was to be subdued by humans. While cutting a few trees to make a cabin or killing enough animals and fish to feed two small families may seem small injury to the environment, it was only a matter of time before the needs of a few gave way to lopping off trees, wildlife, and the earth itself to reach the coal underneath. The pictures I have seen of the devastation in West Virginia could make even the cold-hearted weep. My ancestors saw that land when it was whole and healthy, but they never had its welfare or the welfare of its native inhabitants foremost in their minds.

As you might imagine, the native people of that land, the ones who built the paths and who hunted and fished there freely, were not happy about the new inhabitants. I'm not sure if the Foyles and Tygerts knew they had settled near a well-used path, an extension of the "Warrior Branch," which coming up from Tennessee passed through Kentucky and Southern Ohio, but they would come to pay for their choice.

In early 1754, a band of Native Americans attacked the Foyle's cabin, killing Robert, Elizabeth, and all their children but one, their oldest son. John Foyle, the only family member to survive the attack, happened to be away from the cabin when the violence began. As the story is recorded, John came upon the attack, ran to the Tygert cabin, alerted that family, and escaped with his neighbors back over the mountains to the east. John Files is the man who appears in later records in Virginia.

The Foyle massacre appears in "Lists of Settlers Killed, Wounded or Taken Prisoner in 1754–1758," and a West Virginia historic plaque marks the site.[18] I have known about it for some time. What I did not know until recently is that it is recorded in George Washington's journal of 1754.

GEORGE WASHINGTON

George Washington was commissioned as a major in the militia of the British Province of Virginia in 1753, when he was twenty-two years of age. That same year, he was sent by Virginia Governor Dinwiddie as a messenger from the British crown to "the Comandant [*sic*] of the French Forces on the River Ohio." The two-and-a-half-month trip took Washington as far north and west as what is now Erie, Pennsylvania. At the end of the trip, Dinwiddie asked the young major to write a detailed report, which was published in 1754 as "*The Journal of Major George Washington.*"[19]

At the time, English colonies were lined up along the Atlantic seaboard while the French claimed the vast middle of the continent. A great swath of disputed territory lay in between, running down the western side of the Allegheny and Blue Ridge mountains from what we know as western New York state to the Gulf of Mexico, including most of modern Ohio, Kentucky, Tennessee, and Mississippi.

When Dinwiddie got word that the French were building forts on the Ohio and Allegheny Rivers, that was too close for comfort, and he perceived them to be in violation of treaties and claims that made those territories part of Virginia and Pennsylvania. His letter, which Washington took to the French commander, instructed the French to stop building forts and leave the region.

As you may recall, the French did not comply; and when Washington returned to the area in the spring of the following year, he was fighting in the beginning of the French and Indian War.

In October of 1753, Washington set out for Ohio; this is the part that involves my ancestors. On his return trip, he carried a letter from the French back to Governor Dinwiddie. Near the end of December, Washington and his guide got soaked trying to cross the Allegheny River on a barge they had made and had to spend an extremely cold night on a small island in the middle of the river. He notes in his "journal," "Mr. Gist [the guide] had all his Fingers and some of his Toes frozen, and the Water was shut up so hard that we found no Difficulty in getting off the Island, on the Ice, in the Morning...."[20] He then reports meeting twenty Native American warriors "who were going to the *Southward* to War." The warriors told Washington that when they came upon "seven People killed and scalped, all but one Woman with very light Hair, they turned about and ran back, for Fear the Inhabitants should rise and take them as the Authors of the Murder." Washington continues with a description of the gruesome scene, "the People were lying about the House, and some of them much torn and eaten by Hogs. By the Marks that were left, they say they were *French* Indians of the *Ottaway* Nation, *&c.* that did it."

A footnote to Washington's journal says, "Colonial records indicate the family killed was that of Robert Foyles, including his wife and five children."

Nine
The Waxhaws

William and Martha Simpson settled within the bounds of an area called the Waxhaws, but it took me a while to figure out what that means. In my research on my Simpson ancestors, I kept coming across the place name "Waxhaw" or "The Waxhaws." The first list I ever saw of Jane Simpson's North Carolina relatives was in an article in "The Waxhaw Enterprise." Articles about President Andrew Jackson routinely mention that he was born in "The Waxhaws." I could see Waxhaw, North Carolina, on a map, south of Charlotte, but it wasn't until I really looked at a map and read the geographical description that I began to understand the region.

Growing up in Oklahoma, I was well aware of the Trail of Tears, the long, hard, sad removal of Native Americans to areas west of the Mississippi, specifically the removal of Cherokees from Appalachia to Indian Territory, which is now Oklahoma. I was much more interested in the fact that Andrew Jackson was responsible for this travesty than where he was born. The way I remembered it, he was the jerk who ran all the Native Americans out of the Southeast so people (like his relatives and mine) could have the land.

In fact, he did run most the Cherokees out of the North Carolina mountains, but he had grown up in an area that had very few native people left by the time our people, the Scots-Irish, arrived.

"The Waxhaws," a kidney-bean-shaped area just south of Charlotte, spreads over two states (North Carolina and South Carolina) and three counties (Union and Mecklenburg, North Carolina, and Lancaster, South Carolina). It is best understood, however, when we stop paying attention to state lines and focus on geographical regions. The Waxhaws are bordered on the east by Monroe, on the west by the Catawba river, on the north by Charlotte, and on the south by Lancaster, South Carolina. Once I drew the boundaries of the region on a map, I could see it included the area of North Carolina where the Simpsons lived. Being generally made up of forests, fields, and gently rolling hills, it included the beautiful landscape I had admired when I visited my ancestors' graves.

The region takes its name from the previous inhabitants, a Native American tribe called the Waxhaws. By the 1750s, the native people had been all but wiped out by smallpox and war. In 1751, half a dozen Scots-Irish families settled near present-day Waxhaw in Union County, North Carolina.

The first church built in the South Carolina part of the region, sometime between 1752 and 1755, was the "Old Waxhaw Presbyterian Church." The Presbyterian families grew, intermarried, and some became wealthy off the production of cotton; but by the 1830s, much of the land was worn out. Much of it was red clay.

* * *

I've had red clay around all the places I've lived in central North Carolina. I used to dig up small plugs of soil from my front yard and from the garden in the back, take them to the Agricultural Extension agent in downtown Durham, and ask about nutrients I should add. But I gave it up. The reports always came back the same: add lime. The high clay content in much of the North Carolina Piedmont makes the soil acidic. It also tends to make it gluey when wet and hard as concrete when dry. The best thing to do is to add lime and as much organic material as possible. Some gardeners dig out all the native soil and start from scratch, but I've never been that energetic. I also believe in working with what you've got.

My Scots-Irish ancestors must have had to deal with this clay from the moment they arrived in the Carolina Piedmont. John Lawson, one of the first Europeans to explore the area in 1700, described the soil as "red as blood." At the time, native people were forming it into pots and bowls that could dry in the sun and be baked in a fire. The clay was good for making bricks. As the Piedmont prospered, factories and commercial buildings were built of this ubiquitous local material.

People today often wonder how the soil got to be so red. Geologists tell us the Piedmont is a remnant of giant mountains that formed millions of years ago. As the mountains wore down, many minerals washed away, leaving the iron content exposed to the air where it rusted and stained the soil. Red clay is hard to work. It has slowed travelers, aggravated farmers, frustrated road builders, and stained nearly everything that has touched it from animal hooves and moccasins long ago to blue jeans today.

Better soil could be found along streams such as Crooked Creek and Four Mile Creek. Thousands of years of flooding spread organic material on the ground, enriching the dirt and making it possible to grow better crops. But the soil away from the creeks was stingy. Early settlers had limited sources of fertilizer, and it wasn't long before the soil played out. Many early settlers attempted to grow corn, which depleted the meager nutrients from the clay soil. Later farmers grew wheat, oats, cotton, sweet potatoes, and the cash crops of tobacco and cotton. Tobacco, in particular, was able to survive in the stingy soil.

* * *

By the 1850 census, there were nearly a hundred Simpsons in Union County, and my guess is that they were all related. With large families and poor soil, it became impossible to divide farms to provide a living for all the children, even all the sons. Some people decided to head west in search of better land and greater opportunities. Lots of people actually, including several Simpsons, but that comes later in the story.

Ten

Overmountain Men
Files Valley, Texas, 1950s

It would not be far wrong to call my ancestors prideful people. My grandmother, *Oh Lord*, it was always *her* Scots-Irish family, *her* Presbyterian church, and *her* land that she defended. In this same vein, some would go so far as to say that the Scots-Irish won the Revolutionary War for America.

I have lots of ancestors who fought in the Revolutionary War. I am eligible for membership in the Daughters of the American Revolution (DAR) from so many branches of my family that it makes me dizzy. I'm not all that interested in the DAR, except for the great records they keep, and I don't actually need many of their records, because other female members of my family have applied for membership and done a lot of research before me. But I find it fascinating that I had so many ancestors in North America by the time of the revolution and that the Simpsons were only the last to arrive.

When William and Martha Simpson arrived in South Carolina, many American colonists resented British control and taxation and were already discussing ways to overthrow British rule. The Simpsons and other Scots-Irish left Ireland in part to escape the oppression of the English. I imagine that my ancestors felt deep animosity toward the British in general and their control of the colonies in particular. They came to the British colonies believing they would find enough room to work their own land, grow their families, and practice their faith. I like to think that when they heard talk of revolution, William Simpson would have been interested in joining the fight.

By 1775, William and Martha were living in Mecklenburg County, North Carolina, where Presbyterian ministers were regularly accused of sedition. Rightfully so. I feel quite sure that North Carolina ministers, like Rev. William Martin in South Carolina, would have spoken openly against the British. Rev. Martin's own church was burned by the British in 1780. He was captured, held as a prisoner of war for a time, and later released.

* * *

Though many North Carolinians know something about the Revolutionary War Battle of Kings Mountain, few seem to know much about the role of Scots-Irish mountain men in that fight. When the British major, Patrick Ferguson of Aberdeen, Scotland, threatened to obliterate the Scots-Irish folk living in the Blue Ridge Mountains, he drew nearly a thousand men out of the hills and into the Revolution. They swooped down out of the mountains (if you can describe walking through mountainous terrain as swooping), fought like the ornery backwoodsmen they were, and contributed to the ultimate American victory.

What drew the mountain men out of the hills and into the fighting in the Carolinas was an earlier threat made by Major Ferguson. In the fall of 1780, Ferguson released a prisoner of war and sent him over the Blue Ridge with the message that unless the mountain militias would "desist from their opposition to the British arms, and take protection under his standard," Ferguson would "march his army over the mountains, hang their leaders, and lay their country waste with fire and sword."[21]

Bloody hell he would! The enraged mountain men from Ulster County weren't going to wait for Ferguson to find his way across their mountains. They vowed to find the lout and teach him a lesson he'd never forget. Fired up by the preaching of Presbyterian clerics, they took out over the mountains, ever after to be known as the Overmountain men. They traveled south from Abingdon in the mountains of Southwest Virginia down into Tennessee, then east into North Carolina and south again to Upper South Carolina. It took them more than two weeks, their numbers swelling as others joined in along the way. There were nearly a thousand of them by the time they made camp just below the South Carolina border, about sixty miles west of Charlotte.

On October 6, 1780, Ferguson was only about thirty miles (a day's march) west of Charlotte and the safety of Cornwallis' troops, when he decided to make camp with his troops (about 1,100 men) on a thin wooded ridge known as Kings Mountain. The rocky outcropping seemed a good spot and might have reminded him of the rock of Edinburgh on which the castle stands. It would have been a fine position in any conventional war, but Ferguson was an ocean away from conventional combat.

Thirty miles further west, the Overmountain men got word of Ferguson's position, and sent nine hundred men through rain and dark of night to reach the British forces on October 7. That afternoon, the Ulstermen made a surprise attack, scrambled up the side of the embankment, whooping and hollering all the way. Imagine nine hundred angry Hatfields and McCoys, coming at you through the woods. These men were tough as shoe leather and mad as hell. Many were first-generation settlers from Ulster and fierce in their commitment to their found freedom. James Webb describes their military style in *Born Fighting*.

> Under the militia concept their command structure fell
> somewhere between loose and nonexistent—John Sevier,
> one of their leaders, "gave his commands as to equals, and
> because his orders appealed to his men as being wise and
> practical, they gave unquestioned obedience." Another
> commander, Isaac Shelby, told the militiamen that once
> combat ensued, "don't wait for the word of command. Let
> each one of you be your own officers ... availing yourselves
> of every advantage that chance might throw your way.[22]

Ferguson lined up his redcoats and commanded them to shoot in orderly volleys. The British troops were no match for guerrilla fighters, many of whom were from Ballymena and Ballymoney, like William Simpson. They were sturdy mountaineers who had carved a livelihood out of the wilderness and fought off the Native Indians to do it. The Overmountain men won soundly in just over an hour and might have slaughtered every last one of the surrendering soldiers had their own leaders not restrained them.

Knowing that Cornwallis was nearby and might be on his way, the Patriots cleared out after their victory. The men from the mountains headed home to tend to their farms and families and defend the frontier against its native people.

The victory at Kings Mountain galvanized the opposition to the British, and soon other Ulstermen in the region joined the fight. They formed militias. Three months later, in January 1781, this newly formed band of Patriots faced the British again at the Battle of Cowpens. The night before the battle, such a heavy frost set in that some of the Scots-Irish soldiers woke the next morning to discover that their hair had frozen to the ground. That didn't stop these sturdy men from going on to win the battle that day.[23]

I believe that both my Simpson and Files ancestors fought in that battle. They may have served under Daniel Morgan, who placed his regulars and local militiamen from Georgia, South Carolina, and North Carolina, between two rivers, to encourage the volunteers not to run away when the fighting began. He also used them wisely by asking them to fire twice, once they were under attack, and then retreat and regroup at the rear. Several times during the battle, Morgan used the Scots-Irish instinct to run hither and yon to unsettle the British forces and win the day. That sort of chaotic behavior on the battlefield was unknown to King George's well-trained soldiers.

If you think of these mountain men as hillbillies, you'd be right, for that mostly derogatory term has been used to describe the Scots-Irish folk who lived in the Appalachian and Ozark mountains. It may have come from the Scots-Irish affection for King William of Orange, who had defeated the Catholic king, James II of England, in the Battle of the Boyne in Ireland in 1690. "William" and "Orange" remained important terms for the Scots-Irish in America. Orange Presbytery, which had been formed in 1770 and was one of the oldest and largest of the presbyteries in the South, ordained me as a Presbyterian minister in 1977. At some point in American history, Billy's boys came to be called hillbillies, though probably not as early as the 1780s.

The British defeats at the Battles of Kings Mountain and Cowpens foiled their plan for winning the war. They had hoped to capture the South and to use their position in the South and their troops in the North to trap and squeeze George Washington and his troops.

But they failed to get a solid footing in the South. Many say the King's war was lost from this point on.

We all know the eventual outcome. Cornwallis gathered his forces at Yorktown, where Washington's troops laid siege. With no reinforcements in sight and a position that was increasingly untenable, the British commander surrendered on October 19, 1781. King George's fleet arrived five days too late to be of any assistance. Seeing the much larger French fleet that had come to the aid of the revolutionaries and hearing of the surrender, the British ships turned and sailed away.

Eleven
Graves of My Ancestors

Sally Thomas sent me an email in January 2007 saying that a two-mile stretch of Four Mile Creek was being turned into a greenway. She said there had been an article in the *Charlotte Observer* about it. I was again surprised that she remembered my family's connection to that little stream. When I found the article online, I was delighted with the level of detail and was able to look at maps and find the exact area in southern Charlotte where the work was taking place. I was so happy to learn that concrete culverts were being removed and that the creek was being returned to a natural state. I have always hated the idea of trapping streams between concrete walls or burying them under parking lots. Creeks need to be allowed to meander, to flood, and to change their course over time. If we humans box them in, we block tree roots and wildlife from life-giving water.

In May, Amelia, another friend in the Charlotte area, pointed me to an additional article on the creek. I loved the title immediately, "A Creek Runs Through Us." The article notes that "for early inhabitants, creeks were the foundation of life." Native Americans settled temporarily on the larger creeks and gave their names to many of them. In the 1700s, white settlers built farms and "grew wheat, corn, and cotton on the rich bottom soil."[24]

I promised myself I'd go see some of the land and creeks where my ancestors lived and two years later made good on my promise.

On the first of May 2009, I drove to Charlotte to meet some real live Simpsons and to see our ancestral lands. I had found them in newspaper and TV clips on the Internet about their efforts to clean up the graves of our ancestors, William and Martha Simpson. I made contact with a man called Buddy, who invited me to a family reunion in Charlotte on the first Saturday in May and promised to take me to the cemetery. I arranged to stay with Sally Thomas again, thirteen years after that first trip to the Charlotte library.

Quiet, openhearted Sally Thomas greeted me at her front door, her clear eyes and warm hug assuring me I was welcome. She showed me around the house and helped carry my bags into the guest room. Sally and husband Zack hadn't been in the house long, having bought it when they returned from a few years on the mission field in Guatemala. Their comfortable, uncluttered home had a large screened porch on the back and a vegetable garden beyond, where we found Zack. Supper on the porch included a salad of lettuce from the garden, conversation about shared political interests, and a feeling of being with family.

The next morning, after breakfast, I stopped by a grocery store to pick up food to share at the reunion. I had no idea who would be there or what they ate. Chips and guacamole were always great favorites at gatherings in Durham and easy to pick up. Surely they'd fit in at a potluck lunch. I drove to the appointed spot, wondering all the way about why this Scots-Irish clan was gathering at a Baptist Church. In my reading since then, I've discovered that lots of independent-minded, patriotic folk from northern Ireland migrated to the Baptists and Methodists; but at the time, I was simply puzzled.

The small gathered crowd of about twenty-five seemed familiar, not because they seemed like relatives, but because they seemed like regular North Carolina folk, just like the ones I had met when preaching at small North Carolina churches or accompanying my husband to his family reunions. They didn't look particularly like MamaMay and her siblings, they didn't all have sharp chins, but they all looked like other white Southerners, probably some mix of Scots, Irish, and English. And they had held onto the name. They were Simpsons.

As I asked questions of the older people, I discovered they were descended from William and Martha Simpson's son James, while I am descended from sons John and Thomas. We were cousins, even if distant ones. If I climb up my family tree six steps to William and

Martha and come down another branch about five or six steps, I arrive at these people.

Lunch consisted of lots of Kentucky Fried Chicken and all the fixings. No one touched my chips and guacamole. As I said, they were regular North Carolina people. As a vegetarian, I felt slightly embarrassed, a little hungry, and like an outsider. It was clear that my connection to these folks was not going to be a culinary one.

We had carried on Simpson family traditions in our own ways. They stayed close to the spot where our mutual ancestors lived. I clung to one far-flung Texas branch of the tree and to the Presbyterian part. We shared a passionate connection to the Simpson family, if not to the same denominations or political persuasions, and we appeared to share the Scots-Irish tendency to be stubborn and independent.

* * *

Having made a plan to meet Buddy and some of the others at the Simpson family cemetery in Union County later in the afternoon, I went on my way. Though I had not found my new best friends, I had filled in a few more pieces of the puzzle. I was pleased to have met some Simpsons and to realize how early the ancestral tree branched into distinct families.

I stopped in Pineville, a few miles from the church, to see my friend Amelia, who had recently moved there. After a pleasant hour touring the house, admiring her garden, and chatting with her children, I got back in the car, took the beltline around the eastern part of Charlotte, and then headed further east toward the graves of my ancestors.

Buddy's directions took me on two-lane highways through lush rolling country and finally to a scraped dirt parking area just off the side of the road. The first to arrive, I parked the car and set out on foot. As instructed, I kept my eyes on a flagpole at the back of the field and followed a hard-packed dirt track through a flat open field of stubble. As I walked, I studied the irregular line of trees beyond the flagpole and decided the trees marked the edge of Crooked Creek.

The small graveyard, enclosed by a chain link fence, boasted an American flag, waving from its pole. Two enormous native hollies with pale yellow flowers offered partial shade. There were no standing headstones, but I did notice two broken stones that must have once marked my ancestors' graves. The simple reddish-brown slabs of sandstone had "RTHA SIMPSON" and "WILLIAM SIMPSON" scratched into their flat faces. The front end of Martha's stone was missing, and the rest was broken in two parts. William's was broken into three pieces.

In a matter of minutes, I was joined by half a dozen of my newly found clan. Together we admired official-looking bronze plaques, flat on the ground, that read, "William Simpson, Continental Line, Revolutionary War, 1752–1821" and "Martha Orr Simpson, wife of William Simpson, 1752–1832."

"Who arranged for these plaques?" I asked aloud.

"Reverend Claude," someone answered.

I pressed on, "Who's that?"

"He was a preacher, but he died. He has a son who is a minister in Chapel Hill at a big church." My heart nearly stopped.

"What did you say?"

"His name is Mitchell Simpson."

Mitch Simpson's winning smile, dark beard, and bright eyes flashed to mind. He's the Simpson who was a class ahead of me in seminary in the mid-1970s. There had even been a brief romantic spark between us. Classmates nicknamed the flamboyant Baptist student "the Bishop," and he had done well as a minister. I thought my knees might give way.

There I was standing on land once owned by my ancestors, gazing at the graves of ancestors who came to this country in 1772, and what I found out was not ancient but fairly recent history. I am related to a man I knew in graduate school, one with whom I had more than a passing acquaintance.

Several months later, I called the senior pastor at University Baptist Church in Chapel Hill. He took the call.

I told Mitch I had discovered that we were related and recounted the trip to the Simpson cemetery. I said that when I moved to North Carolina, I often said I was related to all the Simpsons in the state. Though I hadn't really known what I was talking about, it turned out to be truer than I had guessed.

Mitch said his mother was a Union County gal and that she had been involved in the Union County Historical Society. Even though she spent much of her adult life in the central part of North Carolina, she made frequent visits "home." After a few more pleasantries, we said goodbye.

Mitch never had to work at being a Simpson, because he always was one. His father, Rev. Claude Simpson, was born in Union County. They are descendants of the original William and Martha Simpson's son James. I'm descended from *two* of William and Martha's sons, but my ancestors were the ones who moved away. My great-grandmother Jane would almost certainly have known her cousin John Culpepper Simpson, Mitch's great-grandfather, but that's where the familiarity probably stopped. The miles between Texas and North Carolina weakened the family ties.

* * *

After visiting the graves of William and Martha Simpson, I walked back across the open field, got in my car, followed Buddy around to a couple of other gravesites, and then drove around on my own. I snapped pictures of gently rolling countryside and of a street sign that said "Simpson Road." When the road crossed the North Fork of Crooked Creek, I stopped and got out to take a better look. Though I didn't stick my feet in the creek, the flowing water and overhanging trees sure looked inviting. Instead, I got back in my car and headed north on North Carolina Highway 601 and wondered why my ancestors had ever left this lush green land.

Twelve
North Carolina Land

My Texas family believes in holding onto land, acres and acres of land. But I don't live in Texas and never have. I'm not a farmer or a rancher; I'm a lefty feminist living in the People's Republic of Durham. That's why I'm surprised by my own irrational attachment to three pieces of Texas land I stand to inherit from my mother. When I consider ever letting go of the land she inherited from her parents, I notice I'm embarrassed for even having the thought. Something deep within me insists, "Only a fool would do that!" I am not sure I could even find all three parcels by myself, though my grandfather and then my uncle took me to see them countless times. You could call my attachment sentimental, but it feels deeper than that.

William and Martha lived beside a good creek, where the soil was rich, and raised a family that included the three children born in Ireland and eight more born in the Carolinas. Ten of the children lived into adulthood, five daughters and five sons. William survived the Revolutionary War and lived to be sixty-nine years old. Martha lived to be eighty and to know most of her seventy-some grandchildren. The remarkable fertility of my early ancestors is another reason I claim to be related to everyone named Simpson in North Carolina.

Martha's eldest daughter, Elizabeth, married a man named Runnells and moved to Georgia. I have not been able to trace her after that. I have wondered whether Martha and Elizabeth corresponded and whether they would have been able to acquire or afford writing paper. I'm not even sure whether they could read or write. Census data does not include literacy until the late nineteenth century.

The rest of William and Martha's children stayed close by. John, their second child, was one of the most prosperous and is well documented. Because there are so many men named John in this family, I could call this one Rich John or John, Sr., but for now, John will do.

John Simpson was born in Ireland and made the trip across the Atlantic with his parents. He might have recalled it this way:

> My clearest memory of the trip is looking up at billowing sails and lines going every which way. Mother says the food nearly ran out and I complained of hunger. She often said we would all be taller, we first three—James, Elizabeth, and I—except that we nearly starved on the crossing. We played a little game on the ship and for years after the voyage. I'd say, "Mother, where are we going?" She would say, "John, we are going to America." I'd say, "When will we get there?" And she'd say, "When the breath of God blows strong and straight and carries us to the shores of the Promised Land."
>
> When I was an older boy here in North Carolina, she'd ask me where I was going, and I'd say, "To the shores of the Promised Land," when I was only going down the creek to look for crawfish.

* * *

John married three times and had nineteen children. His first marriage to Miss Rogers, in about 1806, produced seven children, six sons and a daughter. After his first wife died, John married Mary Moore and had seven more children, four boys and three girls. I suspect that Mary was the girl next door, since the Simpsons lived next door to a family named Moore, but I have yet to find records to prove my theory. My ancestor Martha was John and Mary's second child and named, I assume, for John's mother. When Mary died, John married Mrs. Mary Polly Estridge and had five more children, the youngest two arriving when he was in his seventies. More than forty years separate John's eldest and youngest children, and about a dozen of his grandchildren were born before his youngest child.

When he died in 1845 at the age of seventy-four, John Simpson left a will (dated 1842) that divided up his property. His wife, Mary Polly, got one third of his land while she lived plus one year's provisions, a bed, some furniture, and a wheeled cart. Sons William, Levi, James, Thomas, Benjamin, and Jackson each got one dollar in addition to "what I have already given them." I assume this means John had already transferred some land to each of them. By 1860, four of them (Levi, Thomas, Benjamin, and Jackson) would each own land worth $1,500–2000, enough for a working farm.

Son Elijah was bequeathed $400, John's sorrel "philly," a saddle, and a bridle. Washington was left $400 plus John's brown mare, saddle, and bridle. (He moved to Arkansas in 1853. We'll get to that story soon enough.) David, who was only fourteen when the will was drafted, got $400, and Peter, who was only a year old at the time, got $200.

John left money to his daughters: Jane $30, Martha $200, Phereby $200, and Elizabeth $200. Sarah and Lucinda were about fifteen years old and not yet married when their father died, so they each got a few hundred dollars, some furniture, a cow and calf, and a saddle and bridle. Daughter Emeline wasn't born until the year after the will was drafted and is not mentioned. The balance of the estate was divided among these sons and daughters: Elijah, Washington, David, Richard, Peter, and Martha.

The upshot of all of this is that John Simpson's older sons got most of his land and the younger children got some money and some items, but not land. Martha, John's daughter and my great-great-grandmother, was already married and had children by the time John made out his will, and she was not given any land. That must have been the custom—to leave land to older sons and not to daughters. She was, however, left a sum of money, which probably helped her family move to Arkansas. And that is how my branch of the family wound up west of the Mississippi.

Martha Simpson Simpson

(1819–1854)

Thirteen

Martha & Pearson

My great-great-grandmother Martha Simpson was seventeen years old when she married her twenty-year-old first cousin Pearson Simpson on September 29, 1836. She became Martha Simpson Simpson. It was not unheard of for first cousins to marry in those days. With so many cousins nearby, most of the boys Martha knew would have been related to her. But when I did the math, I noticed that Martha and Pearson's first child, Catherine, was born only five months after their wedding. That was certainly not what I expected of these strict, buttoned-up Presbyterians. Apparently they were also human.

This somewhat irregular union is the way I came to be descended from *two* of the original William and Martha Simpon's sons. John Simpson, the successful one with all the wives and children, was Martha's father. Thomas Simpson, about ten years younger than John, married Susan Byrd of Rowan County, North Carolina, and had nine children; the third one was Pearson, my great-great-grandfather.

When Martha's successful father John Sr. died in 1845, she was pregnant with Jane. Though she never knew him, Jane and her grandfather John shared an important experience—moving, as children, from the place they were born to a far off land. John, born in Ireland, was not yet two years old when William and Martha sailed for America. Jane would be seven when her family headed west to Arkansas, and Arkansas certainly would have been a foreign land to her.

Constant migration—that's the story of my people, at least for the last few centuries. They went from Scotland to Northern Ireland, from Ireland to the Carolinas, from there to Arkansas and eventually down into Texas. Then my mother moved to Oklahoma, and I moved back to North Carolina. My grandmother MamaMay broke the pattern by being born, living, and dying all in the same state, Texas. Everyone else moved.

* * *

Their moving around was part of the dream of a better life. They moved for land, for space, for a place to raise their children, to make money, and eventually, I'm very sorry to say, to own slaves. They fought wars to hang onto what they wanted. William Simpson fought for freedom from the English. Eighty years later, his grandsons and great-grandsons fought to protect slavery.

Following Simpsons has taught me about how capitalism worked in the early days of this country, how immigrants like the Simpsons got a foothold and eventually made money. The original William Simpson was given land when he arrived from Ireland, a land grant in South Carolina, which he then sold or traded for land in Mecklenburg County, North Carolina. By adding his own labor, that of his sons, and some luck, he was able to accumulate enough property to provide a financial base for his children. But with seventy grandchildren, William and Martha's lands couldn't be subdivided to provide a working farm for all of their children's children, and probably not for my ancestors Martha and Pearson. Martha did receive $200 when her father (John Sr.) died, which may have been enough to buy a farm. The 1842 Union County tax records show that Pearson owned 100 acres.

There were many factors that could have caused people in North Carolina to pack up and make the arduous trip to Arkansas in the mid-1800s, but the main one was the search for land. Owning land was a means of survival, and it also held the possibility of greater fortune. Hanging onto land was so important in my family that my grandmother stopped speaking to one person who bought land away from her relatives. (She did not stop speaking to her relatives, just the outsider who made off with what should have belonged to her family.)

By 1850, Martha and Pearson had eight children, three sons and five daughters, including my great-grandmother Jane. With their fathers still alive, the young family probably lived and farmed along the creeks where William and Martha had settled. Also by 1850, there were hundreds of Simpsons living on Crooked Creek, Four Mile Creek, and Reedy Creeks in Union County, North Carolina, and it was getting crowded!

The land near the Simpson gravesite I visited in rural Union County may seem lush, green, and sparsely populated today, but by 1850 it was crowded and overworked. The soil was giving out. Since owning land was a primary means of survival for people like the Simpsons, moving on to find better soil was a logical next step, at least for some. So, Pearson and Martha, like their ancestors before them, began to listen to the reports of better prospects further west.

Arkansas and Texas were the next, and last, frontiers for the American planter class. Arkansas became a state in 1836 and Texas in 1845. Southern whites moved to the "New South" in droves and took thousands of enslaved African Americans with them. The life they developed would have seemed rough and crude to their settled relations to the east, but they, like their ancestors, were carving what they thought of as a civilized life out of a "wilderness."[25]

A KNOCK AT THE DOOR

(I wonder how long Martha and Pearson considered moving west. If Martha Simpson kept a journal, perhaps she would have recorded that the move to Arkansas began with a knock on the door one afternoon.)

Wednesday, March 16, 1853

It was a sweet Carolina morning. We had come through the worst of the cold, and I even threw one quilt off the bed in the night. Pearson makes so much heat I hardly need thick covers anyway. After breakfast this morning, I sent Ambrose and Lewis out into the yard to start a fire for the wash. Hattie, cousin David Cuthbertson's woman whom he rents out for washing, will be here soon.

We washed—well, Hattie washed and I supervised. Boiling, soaking, and stirring with that big wooden paddle that Daddy threatened to use on us if we pulled peaches off the tree before they were ready. With eighteen of us, there was always somebody getting into trouble. Mama died when I was fifteen, and I took over being in charge of the little ones until Daddy married Mrs. Estridge.

Daddy didn't own slaves. Our kind of Presbyterians are pretty uncomfortable with the practice. My father always said that since we had fought the English so hard for our freedom, we shouldn't turn around and put other people in bondage. He thought we should just send all the slaves back to Africa and let them start over. Sometimes when he said that I wondered if what he really wanted was to go back to Ireland. He was so little when he left there that he doesn't really remember it, but the stories made him long for that misty green place.

I am lucky to have Hattie's help on Wednesdays. She visits eight to ten houses in the neighborhood each week and probably knows more about my relatives than I do. She is a quiet sort who keeps her thoughts to herself, but I know she's listening. I'm careful what I say around her. I was so sorry when David sold her eldest son to a man moving west. I don't even want to think about what it would be like to lose any one of my children. I had to keep an eye on her for a while after that. She was so distracted I was afraid she'd catch her skirt on fire or drop clothes in the dirt.

As Hattie wrung out shirts and pants with her strong hands and dropped them in the big bucket, Jane helped me hang them on the rope. As I lifted each shirt over the line, I said a little prayer for the child who wears it. Sometimes I have to think about which clothes are whose. We pass clothes down the line and the three older girls trade blouses sometimes. We try to make a few new shirts every year, at least one for the big girls, one for the boys, and one for the little ones. As I draped each one over the rope, I secured it with a wooden peg and a prayer. *May our children be healthy. May they grow strong, and may I live to see our grandchildren.*

I stopped for a moment while Hattie wrung out a batch of nightshirts. And looked around at this good land on which we live. Though Pearson says the red clay in the fields is getting weak, there's a wonderful garden patch near the house. The pigs, cows, and chickens seem happy and all eight of the children are well. This is a good place. A healthy place. We are so lucky to live with lots of family around.

Sometimes while working in the yard, I practice reciting the names of my first cousins. There are nearly seventy of us. Pearson has those boy cousins he is so close to, he and his brother Allison. They used to hunt together when they were young and now they help each other with the big chores like shoeing, calving, and harvests.

I feel as happy as I've ever been. I'm not pregnant and the baby is almost three. Easter is on the way, just a week and a half away.[26] A few daffodils by the back door are blooming. It's always touch-and-go this time of year about whether the fruit trees will flower and then get frosted or whether they'll wait. I don't see why the sun and the frost can't get better organized and leave the peach trees alone.

When it began to mist in the late afternoon, the girls and I grabbed the wash off the ropes and took it inside. I had to keep after Jane so she didn't drag a loose sleeve in the dirt. She's such a little thing. At seven she still looks like a five-year-old.

We were still trying to sort the clothes inside when there was a knock at the door. Pearson had come in because of the rain. He had been out checking the fields and was concerned about how much rain we'd had and whether he'd get to plant on time this year.

"Hello," I heard a male voice call from the front of the house. Jane ran to the front door to see who it was and found her favorite uncle, Allison. Jane still gets a kick out of seeing Allison, Pearson's older brother. He was down in Georgia teaching for five years and was like Santa Claus to her, someone she heard about but never saw, and then he became a real person just this year.

"It's Uncle A," she hollered.

"Jane, don't holler in the house," I said as she ran back out to the heaps of laundry. "He has a surprise."

Alison had been staying with his parents since Christmas, when he came to his senses, gave up trying to civilize the wild Georgians, and came on home. I wish he would find him a wife. He's been trying to decide whether to buy a farm, keep helping Thomas in his shingle shop, or what.

Allison came through the doorway waving a letter in front of him, looking as proud as a cat that caught a mouse. Pearson greeted him with their customary bear hug. I always worry one of them really will break the other's ribs doing that.

"This is it, this is it," Allison was almost shouting. I was hoping it was a marriage license or the deed to that farm I heard was for sale over on Crooked Creek, but it was only a letter from a friend of a friend. Allison opened the letter and began to read from the tattered, spotted pages.

> Bears are fat and plenty, deer are plenty and all kinds of game…. The dirt is black as tar, and my yield in corn and cotton this year will be double what it would have been back home.[27]

"Did you hear that? When was the last time you saw a bear around here? There are so many of us around here that we've practically scared off all the deer. We'll be down to eating Carolina Parakeets before long. This is it! This is what I've been looking for! Land is cheap. There's a good road most of the way. Let's go to Arkansas. Let's get the 'pack of boys' and go!"

Allison was red in the face and bouncing slightly on his toes. I'd never seen this bookish man so worked up.

Allison and Pearson are less than a couple years apart in age and close as twins. They did everything together growing up. Pearson, the younger, was more likely to think up a prank or adventure, like jimmying the latch on the pig pen so the pigs got out and wandered around the yard, but it was Allison who figured out the mechanics of the thing. They could be like a two-headed monster when they got to going.

I took in a gasp of air. Evidently I had not been breathing since Allison burst in. Leave North Carolina? Leave all my family to go live in the wilderness with bears and Indians? Drag my children away from the church and civilization and the only two grandparents they have left? That was ridiculous! I wanted Pearson to agree with me.

When I turned to look at my beloved, he was grinning at his brother like they had just been looking at a painting of naked angels. Oh, no. Would this be my last day of peace? Would this be the last spring in my perfect home? Just fold the shirts, Martha. I closed my eyes and said Mama's prayer, "Thy will, not mine, Lord, thy will, not mine."

If we go, I'll take daffodil bulbs to plant by the door.

Fourteen
Curious about the Road

When I used to imagine my ancestors heading west, I'd picture them slogging through mud, hacking their way through dense forests, like Davy Crockett, and making the road as they went. While that was certainly true for early pioneers, my relatives were latecomers, a full generation behind Crockett. Arkansas had been a state for seventeen years by the time my people decided to leave North Carolina in 1853. They reached Arkansas at the height of the cotton boom, but less than a decade before the start of the Civil War, which would bring a screeching halt to dreams of getting rich through cotton production in Arkansas (and anywhere else in the South.) But I'm getting ahead of myself.

Being curious about the road my ancestors might have traveled from North Carolina to Arkansas, I started looking for information about old roads. It didn't take long before I ran across Tom Magnuson and his Trading Path Association. Tom had been studying and mapping Native American trading paths, colonial roads, and stream crossings in North Carolina for decades. When I noticed he was giving a lecture a half an hour away in Oxford, North Carolina, I decided to attend and to ask my friend Ron Moss if he wanted to go with me. Ron was interested in genealogy, and I thought he might enjoy the lecture. It would also give us a chance to discuss an interesting connection between us.

A few months earlier, in February 2008, I had been researching my great-grandmother Ida Moss Wilkirson, my mother's father's mother. I was rooting around in census records to see what I could find, because all I had on Ida Moss was a picture I had taken of her gravestone in the family plot near Grandview, which read, "Ida F. Moss, 1864–1909."

When I looked at the 1900 census, it showed that she was thirty-six years old, living in Grandview with her husband O. L. Wilkirson and several children. The record noted that her father was born in Alabama and her mother in Georgia. I wanted to look further back in time. The 1890 US Census was lost in a fire in Washington, DC, but the 1880 census listed Ida Moss as a sixteen-year-old living in Bell County, Texas, with her parents: father, A. Moss, and mother, D. K. Moss. With a little more digging, I could see that the family was in Alabama in 1860 and in Texas in 1870.

That's when I stopped and wrote my seminary friend Ron Moss, who grew up in Birmingham, "I've just learned that my Mosses were in Alabama. How do you like that? Maybe we are cousins! They left Alabama in the 1860s for Texas."

Ron responded, "Oooooo, Jeanette! I'll be interested to hear more. One of my great-grandfather's siblings (the oldest brother while mine was youngest) left Alabama in the 1860s for Texas!"

I replied, "I see that there are lots and lots of Mosses in Alabama, but I've dug up some names. Augustus Moss took his family to Texas in about 1865. His father was William T. Moss, married to Drucilla. William T. was born in Virginia and moved to Alabama where he farmed and grew old in Talladega County."

Ron responded, "Cousin Jeanette! I'm going to attach a picture of Augustus' wife Kitty." Ron's great-grandfather Flemming Moss and my great-great-grandfather Augustus Moss were brothers. I couldn't believe it. My long-time friend was related to me! And so were his children, whom I adored. We were distant cousins.

Ron had gathered information on the Mosses and made a trip to visit "Summer Hill," the house William Anderson Moss built in 1800 close to the James River, near Amherst, Virginia. Our mutual ancestor, William T. Moss, is thought to be the son of that William Anderson Moss.

Ron sent me a scan of a picture of Augustus Moss' wife, Dorcus Kiturah (D. K.). A note scribbled on the back of the photo says it was taken in Birmingham when "Kitty" was visiting.

I called my mother and explained what I had found. "Grandmother Moss," she said. "Who?" I asked. I had never heard of her. Dorcus

Kiturah "Kitty" Wilson Moss, Mother's great-grandmother, was called Grandmother Moss and was still traveling around when Mother was seven or eight years old. Grandmother Moss would ride the train from Belton, Texas, to Dallas to see her son-in-law, Oscar Lee Wilkirson ("Papa") and his children. Papa was widowed when his wife Ida Moss died of a ruptured appendix and her youngest child was only six years old. Kitty was Ida Moss' mother and wanted to keep an eye on her motherless grandchildren. My mother remembers Grandmother Moss as a cute little woman who was always fun to be around. A family story claims that when Kitty played checkers with her grandson Percy, she'd try to cheat.

Having discovered we were actually related, Ron and I shared some information from our research. He sent a copy of a Moss family history that included a note about Kitty Moss. "She seldom stayed at home for more than a few months without taking a trip to visit somewhere. For the most part these visits were to see her children and grandchildren. She traveled by rail and usually alone. It was not until she was more than ninety years old that she reluctantly acquiesced to the idea that she was too old to travel alone by rail wherever she wanted to go."

* * *

Ron and I left Durham and drove north to the library in Oxford and arrived for the evening lecture on trading paths. Tom Magnuson's explanation of the development of colonial roads was fascinating. Early paths were carefully maintained by Native American—footpaths about eighteen inches wide. They were slightly mounded for drainage and the ground was packed hard as rock by moccasin-clad foot traffic. White settlers were hard on the paths. At first whites used Native American porters to transport goods, but then they turned to pack animals and wagons, which tore up the paths. A person can carry tens of pounds, a pack animal hundreds of pounds, a wagon thousands of pounds. As the carriers got bigger, the roads grew wider and the options for ways to go decreased. A person on foot can go ways a horse can't go, and a horse can go lots of ways a wagon can't go.

Tom's interest in trading paths grew out of his study of military history. He noticed that roads in North Carolina ran from northeast to southwest (think of Washington, DC, to Atlanta) while the rivers run from the northwest to the southeast (as if traveling from Boone to Wilmington). That meant roads are constantly crossing rivers and streams. For armies on the ground, there were few options for crossing, given the numbers of people and horses and the size of equipment. Defend a good crossing, and you've halted an advancing army.

One detail I really liked learning is that you can often find old roads in the woods by looking for stands of daffodils in the spring. Because early settlers needed water and transportation, many built cabins near the intersection of a road and a stream. The women had a habit of planting bulbs wherever they lived. Tom said that if you find a stand of daffodils near a stream in the woods today, chances are you have located an old home site.

My friend Mary Margaret used to bring me a bowl of budding narcissus every year at Christmas time. It was a habit she had picked up from her mother. After Mary Margaret died a few years ago, I bought narcissus for myself and forced them to bloom indoors each winter. I'm not even sure I like them anymore. They grow too tall and leap out of the bowl, blooms, leaves, rocks, and all. But I can't keep myself from growing them. Their presence almost makes my friend live and breathe again.

After the trading paths lecture, I asked Tom about the roads the Simpsons might have traveled when they moved from Mecklenburg County to Arkansas and whether they had hacked their way through the wilderness. Tom disabused me of that notion with something like, "Oh, you'd take that big road that was created for the Native American removal." So, the road was practically a highway by the time my people went west in 1853. And once again, my ancestors benefited from the suffering and removal of native people.

Tom also mentioned a collection of letters and papers in the Duke archives that might interest me. The material included some correspondence from a woman who made the trip from North Carolina to Texas before the Civil War. I made a note to myself to go to the archive at some point to see what I could find. Perhaps it would tell me more about the journey.

Fifteen
Heading West

I know how to get from North Carolina to Arkansas today. I've driven it several times on my way to Tulsa. It's about 800 miles from the Piedmont of North Carolina to Pine Bluff, Arkansas. I can make it in two days if I leave Durham on I-40 and head west. I-40 takes me through Asheville, Knoxville, and Memphis, across the Mississippi on a substantial bridge, and on to Little Rock, where I'd turn south to Pine Bluff.

The road up to Asheville is one of my favorites, with its sweeping curves and amazing vistas across the Blue Ridge Mountains. Much of the road was blasted out of the side of the mountains it hugs. My ancestors had no such mountain highway smoothed out for them, but neither were they wandering in the wilderness. They followed routes that began as paths first laid out by Native Americans, roads that had been used just two decades earlier for the forced removal of native people.

The arrival of Europeans on North American shores began a long history of disasters for native people. Though some of their suffering may have been caused accidentally, as in the case of diseases spread by animals that escaped from the ships of early explorers, most of the destruction of tribal life and the removal of Native Americans from their ancestral lands was intentional. The Trail of Tears, the forced migration of the Cherokees under President Andrew Jackson, is just one cruel chapter in a long history of stunning disregard, treachery, and inhumanity. Thirteen thousand Cherokees made the journey in 1837 and 1838; hundreds died along the way.

Andrew Jackson didn't personally hate Native Americans, but it is hard to tell that from his policies. He was friendly with individual

Indians and took a young Creek boy home to raise along with his white adopted son. Even so, he did not view Native American tribes as sovereign nations; and since whites in Southern states wanted more land, to accommodate them Jackson eventually succeeded in removing most of the Creeks, Choctaws, and Cherokees from the Southeast during the 1830s.

* * *

It was a long and arduous journey from North Carolina to Arkansas in those days. A horse and rider could make it in forty days, covering about twenty miles a day. People traveling with wagons had to be happy with five or ten miles a day, stretching the journey to several months.[28] My ancestors' party of at least thirty white people would have included wagons filled with food, household items, and farming equipment, several horses, and some milk cows. When they lived in Arkansas, some of them owned slaves. So, either they had African Americans with them on the journey, purchased enslaved people in Memphis, or acquired them upon arrival. Pearson Simpson was not a slaveholder in 1850, but by 1860, he is listed as living in Jefferson County, Arkansas, and holding seven slaves.

To avoid the worst of the mountains, when the Simpsons headed west in the 1850s, they probably left Union County and went through the very northern part of South Carolina, across north Georgia, and into Tennessee, crossing the Mississippi at Memphis. Settlers who were headed for Texas would have gone that way as well.

Tom Magnuson said the Simpsons would have taken "that big road" created for the Native American removal. That was probably the road across Tennessee. Another road was built from Memphis to Little Rock in 1838, with much difficulty because the road was supposed to be straight and had to pass "through Swamps, lakes, Bayous, heavy Cane breaks" in eastern Arkansas.[29]

The Simpson party probably started out in the fall and traveled through the coldest months of the year. Immigrants to Arkansas and Missouri were encouraged to come in the cold months so they would have time to get settled before the diseases of the warm months set in. They needed time to clear land and begin planting before the sickly season started.[30]

* * *

Pearson and Martha Simpson and four other white families made the move from North Carolina to Arkansas in 1853, eighty years after the original William and Martha Simpson had arrived in the Carolinas. The five migrating households included four married couples, one single man, and about twenty-three children. The adults ranged in age from twenty-eight to forty-one and included Pearson Simpson and Martha Simpson Simpson; Martha's younger brother Washington Simpson and his wife Margaret Cuthbertson Simpson; Pearson's older brother Allison Simpson, who was unmarried at the time of the move; David Cuthbertson and Matilda Simpson Cuthbertson; and John Simpson (Jr.) and Malinda Hooks.

These people were as interrelated as fingers on clasped hands. Seven of them were cousins. Martha, Pearson, David, Matilda, Allison, and Washington were all first cousins. Washington's wife Margaret was also a cousin, though slightly more distant. John Simpson (Jr.) and Malinda Hooks may have been related to the others, but I have yet to figure out how.

Four of the men were very close in age, born within four years of one another: Pearson, Alison, John Simpson (Jr.), and David Cuthbertson. As boys that close in age, they had probably been friends for a long time, played together at church gatherings and family celebrations from the time they were small. Even though I have no photographs and almost no stories of any of these hardy folk, I have enough historical data to imagine their lives.

A WILD NIGHT

(If Jane Simpson had told a story about adventures on the journey to Arkansas, she might have included this story.)

The wind picked up in the afternoon. We were in a flat area with lots of trees. No hills or mountains like the ones we crossed when leaving what they told me was North Carolina. Cousin Mary and my older sister Sarah and I were walking together, singing some of our favorite hymns to pass the time and take our minds off our feet. My good socks were wearing at the heel, and I had blisters where my feet rubbed against the inside of my leather shoes. These shoes would never be welcome in a church house again. They had dirt and mud in the creases that even the brush I used on Mazie the old mare wouldn't be able to get out.

My skirts were blowing in the dusty wind and while it would be pleasant to have rain settle the dust on this part of the road, none of us liked it when it rained. Thunder made the babies and my little sister Caroline cry. Hard rain soaked our clothes, blankets, wagons, and spirits, and when it came at night, I was too scared to sleep. Back home, my cousin John, who lived on Crooked Creek, told me a story about the time lightning struck his Grandfather Thomas' barn and burned it up along with the hay and one horse inside. John said his father said the ground smoked for three days after. I was afraid of lightning, though I never told Caroline.

The wind was playful at first, but then it became a nuisance. My skirts whipping around made it hard to walk. I had to squint to keep the dust out of my eyes.

We could see the wagons slowing, up ahead. Papa must have decided along with Allison and one of the Cuthbertsons. They were always making the decisions, because Allison was the oldest and wasn't married yet and didn't have a wife and children to pay attention to, or so Papa said. And he had to consult with one of the Cuthbertsons or there would be "hell to pay." (Mama says, "Jane, don't say hell," but it makes no sense to say, "There will be heaven to pay.") Papa might have consulted with his oldest son about whether to stop for the night or risk going a little further, but his oldest children were all girls. I was eight and my oldest brother was only nine. That's why Papa leaned on Allison.

I was thinking about all this when I seed it. (Mama says, "Jane, don't say seed, say saw. But if I see something now, then why can't I say that yesterday I seed it?) Anyway, I saw a dark gray cloud over to the left. I always know left from right because I have a little scar on my left middle finger from when Patch the dog mistook it for part of a biscuit.

On the left, that was South. Every evening Papa reminded us that we were headed West and that South was on the left, where good people lived, and North was on the right, where the greedy people lived, and home was behind us. I liked to stare at his crumpled map when he spread it out on the back gate of the wagon. I can only see the map if he sets me up beside it. When the gate is open, it is even with my forehead. I know because I turned around too quickly one time in the yard back home and hit the corner of it with the side of my head.

Sitting beside the map, Papa points to North Carolina and the road we are on now in Tenny Sea. I'm still looking for the sea, I've never seen one. And then he points to the big open space beyond and says, "That's what direction, Jane?" "West!" I say. I still don't understand the map very well, but I've learned the answer to that question.

So, the dark cloud on the left side of the road—I could see it only when there was a break in the trees. It didn't look like a normal cloud. It was so dark it could have been stuffed with ash and coals, and heavy as the belly of a mare just before a foal sticks its first leg out. I had never seen a heavy cloud like that before. And then the strangest thing happened. The cloud started heading for the ground. Not right near me, but over past the trees somewhere. Part of the big ole mean black cloud started sagging into sort of a triangle shape and pointing to the ground.

I've seen clouds all my life. I used to watch big puffy white ones with my grandmother, Mama Sue. We'd sit on her porch so we could keep an eye on the big pans of peaches baked in the sun. She said that in Ireland, where my great-grandmother came from, it was never hot enough to cook peaches like that. I'm not even sure if they had peaches in Ireland. We'd sit there making sure that the dogs and vermin didn't attack the big flat tin pans atop the wash table and we'd glance up at the summer clouds and make up tales about their funny shapes. This one looks like a giant bunny rabbit being chased by Santa Claus. Stuff like that. But I have never seen a cloud look so mean before.

That dark gray cloud was lowering part of itself down toward the earth and the people on the road started screaming and running off into the trees. Sarah, she's my big sister, Sarah saw someone up ahead waving his arms like he was trying to tell us to get off the road. Just then it started to rain. Hard. Big drops made dust splatter all around us. Before I knew it, my dress was soaked. I was thinking about how I hoped Mama would get something dry out of the chest tonight so I wouldn't have to sleep in damp clothes when Sarah grabbed my arm and jerked me to the side of the road. Sarah, cousin Mary, and I huddled next to the base of a big oak. The wide trunk provided a little bit of shelter from the stinging rain.

I bet we looked silly squatting at the base of that tree, like we were telling secrets or looking for a hairpin that had fallen out. With my head down, my pigtails guided little streams of water to the ground in front of me and I noticed something shiny. A green and brown bug had picked the same spot to wait out the storm. That bug was the last thing I saw for a while. The wind was so loud and the rain so fierce that I closed my eyes and grabbed my knees and said the Lord's Prayer.

Next thing I knew, Sarah was grabbing my arm to get my attention. Everything had gotten real quiet and she said we could get up. I was soaked and my dress was so heavy that when I stood up, it tugged at my shoulder like a baby.

Sixteen
Arkansas Land

The United States acquired the area that would become Arkansas in 1803 along with the rest of the Louisiana Purchase. This acquisition included thousands of acres along the western bank of the Mississippi River. Ten thousand years of flooding created an alluvial plain around this great river, which contains some of the most fertile land in the world.

"The Delta" runs along the eastern side of the river from Memphis, Tennessee, down to Vicksburg, Mississippi. Sometimes called "the Most Southern Place on Earth," the Delta is famous for its good cookin', great music, and high concentration of African Americans. It is known for its nineteenth-century plantations and its violent treatment of African Americans ever since.

Since Eastern Arkansas is just the other side of the Mississippi, Southeastern Arkansas could be considered part of "the Delta," but it is never referred to that way. It's Arkansas. Still, the white people's goal on the western side of the river was the same as in the Delta: grow cotton in the fertile soil and get rich.

European explorers gave the Arkansas River its modern name when they encountered it in 1673. Over then next century, French and Spanish settlers ventured up the Arkansas, some intermarrying with local Quapaw women and leaving descendants. One such explorer was Joseph Bonne.[31] When the river flooded in 1819, Bonne and his wife moved upstream to the first bluff they could find. Their settlement in the dense pine forest eventually became the town of Pine Bluff. Forty years later, when my ancestors arrived in the area, Pine Bluff was a flourishing small town surrounded by good land. Just sixty miles upriver from the mouth of the Arkansas, Pine Bluff marks the western edge of the alluvial plain.

Though Arkansas grew from a population of 14,000 in 1820 to nearly 210,000 in 1850, the area around Pine Bluff remained a rugged and sparsely populated area for decades.[32] One historian, writing of an Arkansas settler who arrived in 1845, explains that "even in the relatively well-settled Arkansas River valley in Jefferson County, his nearest neighbor was three quarters of a mile away, some twenty families were within five miles, and the only town, Pine Bluff (which had two taverns, five stores, one blacksmith, and a boat landing) was eight miles to the north. So, even top planters faced horseback travel, stays in farmhouses that took in travelers, and occasional nights under the stars."[33]

Cotton fed the growth of Southeastern Arkansas. The invention of the cotton gin in 1793 made growing cotton more viable and much more profitable. Demand for cotton goods in Europe and Great Britain was rising, land in the Old South was playing out, so farmers headed further south and west in search of land. The profitability of cotton drove huge numbers of whites to seek land in the Deep South and Texas.

Obtaining land in Arkansas was not difficult. "Public lands were sold to settlers for around $1.25 an acre, with a variety of inviting deals: Buyers could pay for land over several years or pick up tax-forfeited lands for cheap. In 1850, Arkansas began offering swampland to settlers for as little as fifty cents an acre, if the buyer agreed to build levees. By 1859, more than three million acres had been distributed under this program."[34]

The lowlands near the Mississippi and Arkansas Rivers were so swampy, unpleasant, and full of mosquitos that white people would hardly agree to live there. Many chose to locate their farms in somewhat higher areas where the soil was only slightly less fertile. That's the choice the Simpsons made when they settled about fifteen miles from the Arkansas River, near Pine Bluff, in Jefferson County, on the western edge of that vast alluvial plain.[35]

Clearing land and preparing it for planting was hard, hard work. Martha and Pearson probably arrived by oxcart with their children and probably a few slaves in the early months of the year. Together they would have worked to clear the land, while camping out in a crude lean-to. First they likely cleared a small plot for corn and vegetables. Then they built a cabin of logs from trees cut to make the garden plot.[36]

* * *

Typical small-scale Arkansas farms like the Simpson's had two or three field hands or slaves. Enslaved African Americans and white family members worked side by side clearing land, planting, working the fields—adults, teenagers, and any children big enough to help. Farmers aimed to grow all the food and fiber required for both humans and animals. Crops would have included corn, oats, wheat, potatoes, beans, and peas to feed white and black families, while livestock foraged for themselves. Livestock would have included chickens, pigs, milk cows, cattle (and maybe sheep) for milk, butter, cheese, and slaughtering, butchering, and curing meat. Eventually there would also be fruit.[37]

While getting the farm started, they might have survived on wild game and bought or borrowed cornmeal and bacon from neighbors with more established farms. The woods were full of possum and squirrel, deer and bear.[38]

The goal was to settle the family and get a cotton crop in as quickly as possible in late May or June of the first or second year. Growing cotton was different from farming in North Carolina. Turning a profit often required more labor than one family could provide. Using slave labor would have been part of the plan all along: move to Arkansas, buy land for cheap, buy slaves, and raise cotton. Buying slave labor there was expensive. My guess is that Pearson either brought three or four African Americans from North Carolina or purchased them in Memphis.

Simpson landowners had held few slaves while in North Carolina. For example, the 1850 census shows only three Simpsons in Union County who owned slaves: David, Benjamin, and Jackson. I'm not sure how any of my ancestors rationalized buying other human beings, but I suspect the allure of King Cotton and the possibility of getting rich was a temptation that some of them couldn't resist.

By 1860, Pearson owned $3,000 worth of real estate and $4,500 of "personal estate" in Whiteville Township, Jefferson County, Arkansas. The calculated "value" of slaves was included in the "personal estate" figures. The "Slave Schedules" of the 1860 US Federal Census show Pearson as the "owner" of seven slaves, four females ages twenty-five, twenty, four, and three and three males, ages twenty-three, thirteen, and two.[39]

As demand rose and the price of slaves skyrocketed in the western cotton states, enslaved black families in the Old South were visited with a new and unexpected horror. Families were torn apart as white masters sold off portions of families to the new cotton farmers in the west, leading to the largest forced migration in US history. More black people were forced from the Old South to the new cotton states than had been imported from Africa. In the eighteenth and nineteenth centuries, half a million people had been ripped from their African homelands, forced to endure the Middle Passage, and sold as chattel in what became the United States. In the seventy years between 1790 and the beginning of the Civil War, one million black people were torn from communities and families in the Old South and sent or sold to the expanding cotton farms to the south and west.[40]

MARTHA'S DIARY

(If Martha Simpson Simpson kept a diary, she might have made an entry after arriving in Arkansas that went something like this on the occasion of her oldest daughter's birthday.)

February 27, 1854, Catherine's seventeenth birthday

It is cold in this cabin, but how fortunate we are to have a cabin. People who arrived in this part of Arkansas twenty years ago had nothing. This little building can be a work shed when we get our house built, but for now it keeps the wind out and the rain. With ten of us, we at least stay warm, stretched out on blankets cheek by jowl. When the fire in the stone fireplace goes out in the middle of the night I am so grateful we packed lots of quilts. I must say, I miss my reliable black cast iron stove that rarely burned out overnight.

I was born into a settled family, near a generous creek. Free people. My grandfather fought in the war for freedom from the British. My father had three wives, nineteen children and 1,000 acres of land. Mother died when I was twelve. I miss her every day.

I am so grateful that we made the trip from home alive. Safe. Reasonably healthy Lewis broke his arm trying to imitate a turkey vulture, swooping off the back end of a wagon. Sarah had heavy bleeding one rainy day in Tennessee, and I thought she'd ruin every skirt she had on before we got it taken care of. Jane has finally stopped complaining about leaving her cousin John. I hope she learns to like her cousins who moved with all of us.

This seems like a healthy place. We are far enough from the river that people say the ague is not as bad as it is in Pine Bluff or downstream. We can build a house and plant crops and raise a barn before the sickly season sets in on us in late summer. They say it can be pretty bad, but once you get through it, you are sturdy enough to live here. God has not brought us this far to leave us now.

SEASONING

Martha Simpson Simpson died in Arkansas in 1854 at the age of thirty-five, leaving behind a grieving husband and eight children ages five to seventeen. I wonder whether losing his wife so soon after arriving in Arkansas made Pearson regret the decision to move the family. I'll never know. They were aware of the risks, and they were sturdy people.

My great-grandmother Jane was only eight when her mother, Martha, died. I've often wondered how the loss affected the little girl, especially since it was compounded by being separated from so many relatives in the move west. I also wonder how the loss affected Jane's daughter May, my grandmother. I'm interested in the broken places in family stories. I lost my father to divorce at twelve and death when I was twenty-four, and sometimes I think I barely survived those heartbreaks. For many years, I tried to act like it wasn't so bad to lose a father. I got pretty good at denying how hard it was.

When they lost their mother, Jane's older sisters may have told her she had to be brave. Later in life she certainly was. According to my grandmother May, when Jane's husband Frances Marion Files died late in life, instead of focusing on her own sadness, Jane comforted her children. Jane may have learned to absorb the losses through the years—moving, war, losing parents and children. She may have been stoic, accepting, or as a good Presbyterian she may have believed that each departed person had gone to be with Jesus. I've made a point of departing from this family tradition. I cry at funerals and at sad news. My definition of strength includes having feelings and letting them leak out.

All this means that my grandmother May was raised by a mother (Jane) who had lost her mother when she was still a child. Jane had older sisters and eventually a stepmother, but that wasn't the same. She grew into adulthood, married, and gave birth without the presence or support of her mother. I have created a collage in my head of Jane as an old woman lying in her bed, so small that she hardly makes a bump under the covers, with the younger Jane sitting quietly beside her, both bearing up under the trials of the years and drawing comfort from a long line of sturdy women who came before them, women who crossed oceans and continents with their menfolk in pursuit of what we now call the American dream.

I was curious about how Martha might have died, what might have killed her, and found some clues in *The Health of the Country* by Conevery Bolton Valencius. In this fascinating study of immigrants to eastern Arkansas and Missouri in the mid-1800s, Valencius examines commonly held beliefs about what constituted healthy land and explores the settlers' health challenges and practices. The most likely culprit in Martha's case is the malaria that infected so many who settled in the low-lying regions along the rivers.

Two forms of malaria plagued the settlers near the Mississippi and lower Arkansas Rivers at that time. One killed 5% of people who contracted this disease, and the other killed 20–40% of its victims. The dividing line between these two types was roughly the 35th Parallel with the more virulent strain to the south. In moving to Arkansas, the Simpsons moved south of that line.

Martha and Pearson would have been advised to travel in the winter in order to get settled before the "sickly season" set in. Most immigrants to this region, whites and blacks alike, were stricken with the "ague" or "chills and fever," now understood to be malaria. This "seasoning" was an accustomed part of the acclimation to this area of the western frontiers. Those who survived the first bout of the shakes and fever would later endure recurrences of the ailment with somewhat weakened systems, but they usually lived. The Simpsons settled on higher ground some distance from the river. This did not save everyone from becoming infected, but it did lower the morbidity rate.[41]

Physicians of the day didn't understand that malaria was spread by mosquitoes carrying a microscopic parasite and recommended a variety of precautions such as "flannel undergarments, bland and cautious diet, careful avoidance of all raw or undercooked food, sufficient sleep, cool houses and cool drinks, and temperance with respect to liquor and spirits."[42]

Malaria is most dangerous for the very young, the elderly, and women who are pregnant or nursing. Martha Simpson Simpson was only thirty-five when she arrived in Arkansas. Her youngest child was three years old, so she probably wasn't nursing, but she might have become pregnant in the first half of 1854, contracted malaria in August or September, and not survived. She was the only one in her immediate family who died during their first years in Arkansas.

THE SIMPSON CHILDREN

I already knew a lot about Jane Simpson's life, but what of her siblings? I wanted to find out what happened to Pearson and Martha's children after the family moved to Arkansas. By studying maps of Arkansas land grants, I discovered that Pearson's oldest daughters married men who owned land nearby, which makes sense. Who else would they have known in a place they had only lived for a few years?

Pearson Simpson and Martha Simpson Simpson had eight children: Catherine, Mary Ann, Sarah, Ambrose, Lewis, Jane (my great-grandmother), Caroline, and John W.

Catherine, the oldest, was the first to marry. She was eighteen years old when she and Johnson Trucks got married on August 23, 1855. At five feet and ten inches tall, with dark hair, blue eyes, and a dark complexion, Johnson Trucks may have been a good-looking man. I have found no pictures. He was from a big family in Bibbs County, Alabama, southwest of modern Birmingham. The family name appears in records sometimes as Trucks and other times as Trux. At some point, Johnson migrated to Arkansas, and by November 1850, he was farming in Jefferson County with William Ray, also of Alabama. They could have been friends or cousins. The same month the census taker recorded Trucks and Ray, Johnson married Elizabeth Moore, also a resident of Jefferson County. Apparently, Elizabeth died within a few years, because in 1855 Johnson married Catherine Simpson. Catherine was a resident of Jefferson County and Johnson Trucks of Bradley County (which is modern Cleveland County and just to the south of Jefferson County.)

Johnson Trucks bought land in 1859 and 1860, mostly in Bradley County, where he and Catherine lived when they were counted in the 1860 census. Also listed were their two children, Mary Georgie, born in 1856, and Madison, born in 1859. While Madison disappears from the records, Mary Georgie married a man named May, and her descendants can be found in records today.

When Catherine's father, Pearson, and most of her siblings left the state during the war, the Trucks family stayed behind. Perhaps it was because the Trucks had been in Arkansas longer and were more committed to the place. Perhaps it was because they hesitated, and then Johnson Trucks was conscripted into the Confederate Army in 1864. Or perhaps the Trucks stayed because Catherine was already dead. She, like her mother, died and was laid to rest in Arkansas. I don't know what killed her, only that she died sometime before 1870 when the records show Johnson Trucks alone with his children. He married again in 1871.

It wasn't just the Simpson children who were beginning to marry in the 1850s. After Martha Simpson died, Pearson married Henrietta

Savage Byrd on December 11, 1856. Henrietta was a twenty-four-year-old widow with a five-year-old son named Charles. When they married, Pearson had seven children at home, evenly spaced at six, eight, ten, twelve, fourteen, sixteen, and eighteen years of age. His new bride was only six years older than his eighteen-year-old daughter Mary Ann. Pearson and Henrietta had three children together. Ben, their first, was born at the end of 1858, two years after they married.

The following year, Sarah and Mary Ann Simpson, the second and third of Pearson's five daughters, got married. Sarah Simpson chose John Marion Davis, a widowed physician who owned land just a few miles from her father's place. She and Dr. Davis were married on the first of May 1859. At forty-three years of age, Dr. Davis was twenty-four years older than his bride and a couple of years older than her father. Sarah was nineteen when she joined the Davis household and took over the care of two children. She and the doctor would go on to have eight more children of their own, relocate to Texas, help to establish the town of Blooming Grove, live long lives, and leave many descendants sprinkled around the Lone Star state.

The records on Dr. Davis are confusing, but I finally figured out that he had two wives named Sarah. The first one, Sarah Jane Lewis, died, and then he married Sarah Simpson. Shortly after I sorted that out, I discovered that Sarah's sister Mary Ann married a man who had two wives named Mary.

Mary Ann Simpson was twenty when she married Henry Lily Parker in July 1959. He was five years older and a North Carolina native from Davie County, about sixty miles north of the Simpsons' home place in Union County. While it is unlikely that the families knew one another previously, these North Carolina folk had a way of finding one another as they moved west across the country.

As of the 1860 census, Henry and Mary Ann Parker were in Talladega Township, Jefferson County, Arkansas, with Sarah F., their three-month-old daughter. (Henry and Mary Ann would have one more daughter, Wincie C., two years later.) Mary Ann's twelve-year-old sister Caroline was living with them, probably there to help with the baby. Caroline gets counted twice in the 1860 census, once at her father's house and again at her sister's house, but after that she completely disappears from the records.

Henry and Mary Ann Parker eventually moved to Texas, as did many of the Simpsons. Mary Ann died sometime after the birth of her second daughter, and Henry Parker married Mary Jane McCullough in March of 1869. He and Mary Jane went on to have at least six more children. In 1880, Henry and Mary Jane were farming in Ellis County, Texas. The Texas Historical Society's Handbook says H. L. Parker was one of the original settlers in Byrd, Texas. That's in Ellis County, near Waxahachie where my mother was born. It seems that Byrd never grew to be as large as Grandview or Blooming Grove, but not every place could.

I don't know what happened to Henry and Mary Ann's oldest daughter, but Wincie appears in the 1880 US Census—married to a man named Powell and living in Navarro County. She is mentioned in her father's will, as are her sons, Adolphus and W. A. Powell.

I'll tell you more about Pearson's sons, Ambrose and Lewis, in the upcoming chapters about the war. At this point I just want to note that as I worked through the details about Jane Simpson's siblings, I noticed that the members of her family were pulled apart from one another in the 1850s and 1860s. Moves, marriage, war, and death separated them from one another. I began to suspect that this scattering may be part of the reason that I knew so little about them.

Seventeen
War in Arkansas
1860–1862

For most of my life, I have had very little interest in military history and have turned away from conversations about the Civil War. But following one thread of the Simpson's story led me into a corner of Civil War history that held my attention.

Jane Simpson's older brothers, Ambrose and Lewis, were both in the Confederate army, as were her father and the man she would eventually marry. Because the terror, suffering, deprivation, and heartbreak of the war were all around her, I needed to understand this part of the story. It turned out to be more complicated and more interesting than I had suspected.

By 1860, the Simpsons were settled on their farm southwest of Pine Bluff. Martha had died, Pearson had remarried, and his three oldest daughters had found husbands. We can assume that the family, supported by the forced labor of at least four adult slaves, was managing to produce a modest, but possibly profitable, cotton crop. The married-in husbands were nearby, and this small cluster of families would have helped one another on their various farms as needed.

Not only was Pearson's cotton production going well, but grandchildren started to arrive. Catherine Simpson and Jackson Trucks had two daughters by 1859. Mary Ann Simpson and Henry Lilly Parker had one in 1860 and one more after the war started in 1862. Sarah Simpson and John Marion Davis were married and living with one or two of his small children and were preparing to have children of their own. It must have seemed to Pearson that life in Arkansas was going to work out just fine. With friends and relatives at hand, he probably thought he could live out his days in their new frontier home. Except for constant change in the makeup of her family (losing her mother to death and several sisters to marriage), Jane was probably beginning to feel somewhat at home in the West. As the oldest daughter at home, she would have been busy caring for younger children.

But it was not a stable system. The profitability of cotton depended on the forced labor of African Americans, and although that evil and inhumane system might have continued a few more years, the abolitionist movement in the United States was strong, as was the pig-headed belligerence of Southern politicians.

The election of Abraham Lincoln in November 1860 brought the conflict between the North and the South quickly to a head. Southern politicians saw the election as both a defeat and a challenge. In South Carolina, they passed a secession act in December 1860; six other Southern states followed suit in the next few months.

North Carolina and Arkansas waited to join the Confederacy until after Southern forces fired on Fort Sumter in April of 1861, demonstrating the divided opinions among residents of those states and their reluctance to engage in all out warfare. In general, North Carolina and Arkansas citizens were never as enthusiastic about the Confederate cause as people in states with economies more fully dependent on large slave plantations such as Virginia, South Carolina, and Georgia. Union supporters could be found in North Carolina and in Arkansas, and neither state boasted long lists of men who signed up at the first call to arms. Once conscripted, many North Carolina and Arkansas soldiers simply walked away from the fight and were designated "deserters," which I take as a sign of their ambivalence about the conflict.

In order to mount a large enough army to fight the Union, Jefferson Davis and the Confederate Congress passed the Conscription Act in April 1862. It required the enlistment of all able-bodied white men between the ages of eighteen and thirty-five. This would have included Jane's oldest brothers, Ambrose and Lewis, as well as Mary Ann's husband, Henry Parker, and Catherine's husband, Johnson Trucks. As the war trudged on, the increasingly desperate need for soldiers spawned more Confederate conscription acts, which eventually drafted men up to the age of forty-five and later fifty, including Jane's father, Pearson.

When Ambrose and Lewis signed up on May 1, 1862, the war had already come to Arkansas. The Union had won a battle at Pea Ridge in the northwestern part of the state in March that year, which made Arkansas slaveholders increasingly nervous.

* * *

While I was trying to figure out when the various men in the family were drafted and when Jane Simpson's family moved to Texas, I remembered that Tom Magnuson (the guy who studies colonial trading paths) had mentioned some papers at Duke University about a North Carolina woman who lived in Texas during the Civil War. I called the archives and arranged to take a look at the papers.

The letters and papers of Theophilus and Harriet Person Perry are housed at the Rare Book and Manuscript Library at Duke. When the archivist on duty gently handed me a bulging cardboard box of file folders on the day of my visit, I was surprised at the sheer volume of the collection. The first folder held fraying yellowed pages filled with the ornate script I have come to recognize as nineteenth-century handwriting. Some of the 150-year-old pages were so fragile that they were preserved in individual plastic sleeves. I was a bit surprised that I was allowed to handle the delicate documents. After an hour or so of squinting and tilting my head this way and that, I was stumped. Many of the words were illegible, and when I could make them out, I often couldn't understand what Theophilus and Harriet were talking about. They kept referring to "Sister" or "Brother" instead of mentioning their various siblings by name. I needed an annotated chart of their relatives or more background on the nature of families during that era.

I left the library happy to have met Harriet and Theophilus, real people, who had grown up in North Carolina and later lived in Texas. I felt the strain of their wartime separation, but I was discouraged that I might never know much more about them. I went home, Googled their names, and began reading about Harriet Person's family home, Person Place, now a historic site in Franklin County, North Carolina.

Then, as though stumbling across the answer to a prayer, I discovered that Jane Johansson, a military historian, had transcribed the letters and transformed them into *Widows by the Thousand: The Civil War Letters of Theophilus and Harriet Perry, 1862–1864.*[43] Best of all, Duke owned a copy of the book.

I scurried back to the library the following day and snatched the one copy of *Widows* off the shelf as though I had found the last tree for sale on Christmas Eve. I'm not sure anyone else knew or cared about the book, but I was nearly breathless to have it in my possession. Since I had no wartime letters from any of the Simpsons, this felt like the next best thing.

Theophilus and Harriet had grown up in Franklin County, North Carolina, about thirty miles north of Raleigh. When Theophilus' father moved his family to Texas in the late 1840s, Theophilus and one brother stayed behind to attend the University of North Carolina in Chapel Hill. After graduating in 1854, Theophilus moved to Texas, where he set up a law practice and received "ten slaves and 130 acres of land" from his father."[44] He returned to North Carolina, courted Harriet Person, and proposed. After they married in early 1860, Theophilus moved his new bride to Texas, and together they set up housekeeping on his small farm in Harrison County Co., near Marshall, Texas.

Theophilus and Harriet were settling into their new life and starting a family when Theophilus was called up by the Confederacy in 1862 and went off to fight. He spent part of the war near Pine Bluff, Arkansas, very near the area where the Simpsons lived (or had lived).

* * *

With the Confederate defeat at Pea Ridge in northwestern Arkansas in March of 1862, danger was increasing for farmers in Arkansas. Conscription was announced in April; Lewis and Ambrose Simpson mustered in on May 1, 1862, leaving Pearson without two of his stronger farmhands. With the war nearby and talk of slaves escaping to the safety of Union camps, I imagine Pearson might have asked himself whether it was worth planting cotton, which needs to go in the ground in late April or May. He was left with his second wife Henrietta, her eleven-year-old son, four adult African Americans, sixteen-year-old Jane, eleven-year-old-John, and some younger children. His sturdy sons-in-law, Johnson Trucks and Henry Parker, were also called up in 1862, so any assistance they might have provided at planting and harvesting was gone.

If the cotton crops of the late 1850s and early 1860s were good ones, Pearson might have amassed some cash with which to start over in another, safer place. By November 1862, a member of the Texas Cavalry noticed the steady stream of whites leaving Arkansas for Texas, "Every day we meet refugees with hundreds of Negroes, on their way to Texas."[45] Refugees? That seems an odd way to describe relocating farmers, but that's what they were called. In a letter dated February 18, 1863, Harriet Person Perry tells her sister, "I have rented our place to a refugee from the Arkansas river...."[46]

Joining the migration, Pearson moved his family to Texas sometime in 1862, eventually purchasing a farm near Grandview, Texas. During this period, planters took as many as a 150,000 slaves to Texas from Arkansas and surrounding states in an attempt to avoid giving up their "property."[47] The men who ran Texas were happy enough to see them coming; white Southerners had built Texas to be a slaveholding region. In fact, there was a huge fight in Congress over whether to let Texas into the Union, because doing so would increase the slave-holding area of the country by 50 percent. Southern politicians won the argument, and Congress admitted Texas as a state on December 29, 1845. Some say that admitting Texas as a state tipped the scales and caused the Civil War.[48]

A biographical history of Navarro County, Texas, helps to illuminate the underlying impulse behind this migration to Texas. In that book, a biography of Lewis Simpson mentions that his father-in-law, William Cole, "represented his county two terms in the Legislature of Arkansas, was a prominent farmer by occupation, and came to Texas in 1864, to save his negroes." I gasped when I read it. The biography was published in 1893, thirty years after the Emancipation Proclamation. Even so it was clearly still acceptable to uncritically describe the way white people dragged African American slaves out of the way of advancing Union troops and the possibility of freedom as *saving* them.

AMBROSE SIMPSON

I knew that Jane Simpson lost her first child, Ambrose Files, in infancy and had noticed that she named the baby after her brother Ambrose. Since I had no information on the brother as an adult, I assumed that something happened to him and that Jane chose the name as a way to honor this sibling.

The records seemed to support my assumption about his fate. Ambrose Simpson shows up in official records as an eight-year-old in North Carolina in the 1850 census, as an eighteen-year-old in North Carolina in the 1860, and then as a member of the Confederate Cavalry. That was all I knew about him until one morning in January 2011 when I came across a note on Ancestry.com saying that Ambrose died on December 7, 1862, in the Battle of Prairie Grove in Northwest Arkansas. He would have been twenty years old.

By searching Confederate records, I discovered that when Ambrose and Lewis joined up, they were assigned to Clarkson's Battalion in Arkansas, both as privates with horses, making them cavalrymen. In July 1862, they probably moved with Clarkson into Indian Territory, where they would have been involved in the disastrous Confederate defeat at Locust Grove. After that, what was left of their unit was reassigned to Clark's Regiment, where they were serving at the time of Prairie Grove.

* * *

Fourteen-year-old Julia West Pyeatt had a clear view of the terrifying Prairie Grove battle from her family's house on West Hill. "It was a beautiful, cold, frosty Sunday morning," she recalled years later. "About ten o'clock the cannonading began and about noon war began in earnest. When it seems everyone would be killed."[49] Twenty thousand men joined the battle in the hills and fields around Julia's home. Other eyewitnesses recalled the deafening gunfire that resulted in 2,500 casualties. The Union side lost 167 dead, 798 wounded, and 183 missing; for the Confederacy, 300 were killed, and 1,200 were wounded or missing. I imagined Ambrose as one of the young men lying dead at the end of the conflagration, most likely in a pool of his own blood. And what of his brother? Was Lewis by his side when he died?

After the fighting ended, men from the neighborhood, including one who was a doctor, responded to the cries of the wounded and went out into the carnage to help, tending to Union and Confederate soldiers alike. The house on West Hill was filled with Union officers and wounded Yankees. Young Julia reported sleeping very little that night. When the army moved on, the family was left with hundreds of wounded men and very few supplies.

It didn't matter which army showed up at the door, it was bad for families either way. At Prairie Grove, the Yankees killed and ate the cattle, hogs, sheep, and chickens and used whatever was stored in the cellars. They also burned four family homes to the ground. It wasn't much better when the Confederates arrived. They'd take all the supplies, but at least they would leave the homes of loyal Southerners standing.

Months after making this discovery about Ambrose's fate, I ordered *Fields of Blood*, a book detailing the lead up to and battle of Prairie Grove. When it arrived, I read the first forty pages and was surprised how interesting a battle narrative could be. Maps and descriptions made it possible for me to imagine where Clark's men were positioned, exactly where Ambrose and Lewis might have been walking, crouching, or standing. I felt sure I was looking at the spot where Ambrose Simpson died.

* * *

In late November 2011, another resource I had ordered arrived in the mail. This study, *Clarkson's Battalion, C.S.A*, provided a detailed history of the battalion and as much detail as the author could find about each of its men. I found Ambrose and Lewis Simpson in the index and squealed when I read that Lewis was 5'6" and had red hair. I had not pictured him with red hair. I had not pictured him much at all, and certainly not as a short person like Jane Simpson and me.

What of Ambrose? I assumed I'd find corroboration that he died at Prairie Grove in December 1862. But no, the date of death was January 22, 1863. So, maybe he was wounded and died a little later. Perhaps he was carried off the field by little Julia West Pyeatt's father. I read further. Ambrose Simpson, died January 22, 1863, in Little Rock. Cause of death: rubeola. Measles.

What? I had studied the battlefield at Prairie Grove house-by-house and hill-by-hill and created a clear picture for myself only to discover that Ambrose died of measles. That's not the way I wanted the story to go. If he was going to die in the war, I wanted him to die in a famous battle, so I could go visit the battlefield and feel a part of it. Not measles!

Well, there it was—the answer to the puzzle. No one ever told my mother that her great-uncle Ambrose died of measles in the Civil War. She didn't even know she had a great-uncle Ambrose until she read the same family history I did. What bad luck for Jane Simpson to have lost her oldest brother to a wartime disease!

It took me a minute to remember that at the time measles could be deadly. More soldiers were lost from infectious diseases in the Civil War than from combat wounds. Camps were crowded, sanitation was terrible, and contagious diseases that found their way into the camps spread like wildfire.[50]

In May 1863, after the death of his brother, Lewis Simpson deserted the army when it was stationed in Bradley County, Arkansas. He was close to home and probably just walked away. Many North Carolinians were less than enthusiastic about the war and just walked away. But then the threat of violence, arrest, or court martial may have encouraged him to return to the war. He took an oath of allegiance and rejoined the troops in February of 1864. Lewis, unlike his brother, survived the war.

Jane Simpson Files

(1846–1933)

Eighteen
War in Texas

Jane Simpson moved to Texas in 1862 with her father, stepmother, and a few younger siblings. Even though records say she was married near Grandview, Texas, no one ever told me where she and her family lived. Finally, a few years ago when I started asking more questions about the Simpsons, my Uncle Oscar Lee cleared up the mystery. On one of our typical outings to count the cows in a pasture near Grandview, Oscar Lee pointed to a farm on the right-hand side of the road and said, "That was the Simpson Place." We were on a farm-to-market road just east of Grandview. I had ridden past the place hundreds of times with my grandparents or my uncle.

I don't remember my grandmother ever showing me the place or saying, "My mother lived there." She took me to the spots that were important to her: Files Valley and Itasca, where she had grown up. She showed me pictures of her mother but never told me the Simpsons lived so close to Grandview, where she lived and raised her family. My guess is that she didn't point out the Simpson farm, because she didn't have a relationship with it. Her relatives only lived there five or six years before moving forty-five miles away to Blooming Grove.

Pearson Simpson wasn't called up by the Confederates until after he had moved the family to Texas. He was forty-four, too old to be drafted by the First Conscription Act passed in early 1862, which targeted white men between eighteen and thirty-five. But the Second Conscription Act (later in 1862) raised the age limit to forty-five and included Pearson. Since the second act was not implemented until July of 1863, I expect Pearson had time to get the family settled and to plant some crops before he had to go. He was assigned to Company A, 20th Infantry Regiment (also called the 20th Battalion), Texas State Troopers.

Pearson might have preferred the cavalry, as many Texans did. Historian Charles Gear points to "the disproportionate number of mounted units from Texas in the Confederate army."[51] According to my great-grandfather, Frank M. Files, "It was almost impossible to get a Texan to join the infantry." He claimed, "The only way they got some of them was to organize a cavalry troop and then dismount them. And, believe me, they sure did kick up when they found they had been tricked."[52]

Theophilus Perry's letters home from the war offer glimpses of military life. In December 1863, he writes of the cold and rain, of suffering from constipation, and of provisions he feels lucky to have.

> I am messing with Nathan Ward, who is Captain Quartermaster in our Regiment. We agree finely and live as well as camps will permit. This is a land of sugar. We have coffee to drink. It cost 10 dollars.... Provisions are not so scarce, but confederate money is almost worthless.[53]

> I had a goose for dinner, some of the Peaches you sent stewed and some beautiful candied honey. The honey was made out of sugar by the Bees, and is very fine. I bought 13 pounds at one dollar a pound. All of the Lard mother sent is gone. I have Bacon & flour enough to last one month. Nathan has paid for half the Bacon & flour.... I opened the Sugared Pears & Figs you made for me the other day. They are excellent. I have lost the little bag of Peaches, or never brought it from home. These little delicacies make me think of my happy home.[54]

Meanwhile, Harriet Person Perry's letters to her husband show bits of daily life on an East Texas farm, which would have been similar to life for the Simpsons. In one letter, Harriet says she was unable to attend a social gathering in town, because she was putting in a garden. In another, she is proud of how many garments she had made out of some cloth that had been given to her.

I have tried to imagine what life on the farm was like for Jane, a young woman of eighteen. Her mother was dead, her father and two older brothers had left for the war, one brother was already dead, and her three older sisters were married and lived elsewhere in Arkansas or Texas.

There were probably six white Simpsons and seven black people left on the farm near Grandview while Pearson was away. Jane's stepmother, Henrietta, would have been in charge of her blended family, which included Jane, two boys close to fourteen, and two little children. The black people, whose names I do not have, included two women in their twenties, two black men (seventeen and twenty-seven), and three children under the age of nine. That's enough people to run a small farm—put in a garden, milk a cow, gather eggs, and chase the fox from the hen house—and it seems like they could have at least fed themselves.

Before the war was over, three quarters of the draftable white men in the South served in the military. As Drew Gilpin Faust points out in *Mothers of Invention*, "with the departure of so many men to the battlefield, the Confederate home front became a world of white women and of slaves."[55] Letters and diaries written by white women in the overwhelmingly rural South of the 1860s show that these women took on physical labor, farm management, and decision-making roles that would change them forever. One unintended consequence of the war was that many white farmwomen and owning-class women acquired skills and a certain amount of self-reliance that had been unavailable to them before.[56]

One troubling question is who enforced the hideous institution of human bondage when the white patriarch was gone. Who made the decisions about when to plant and when to harvest? The responsibility would have fallen to Henrietta, Jane's stepmother, though the expert knowledge about farming probably belonged to the black people.

Our romantic notions of everyone "pulling together" to survive hard times may kick in at this point, but they are romantic, at best, and mostly intended to ease white guilt. Yes, some white people and black people felt a measure of fondness for one another in the slaveholding South, but that did not change the fact that the black people were held in place against their will, without pay for their work, and with the constant threat of violence. Hard times changed none of that.

Some white women found themselves unable to cope with the unaccustomed burden of running a farm without the presence of white men. Newspaper editorials and legislation addressed the problem of white women trying to manage farms and especially slaves on their own.

Harriet Person Perry struggled and then gave up trying to manage the farm, telling her sister,

> I broke up housekeeping last week & moved to Mr. Perry's Father's to live—I tried living alone seven months & became so tired & dissatisfied I concluded it would be best to break up. I have rented our place to a refugee from the Arkansas river & shall hire out the negroes—the[y] would not work for me....[57]

Whatever the human relationships were like on the Simpson farm in 1864, we can be sure that they were not a bunch of happy campers marooned on Gilligan's Island trying to work things out in equitable ways. The household depended on chattel slavery with all its cruelty, injustice, and inhumanity. And the white women were in charge.

I have wondered how these years shaped Jane's attitude toward African Americans. About the only clue I have to Jane's relationship with black people is something that happened when I was about fourteen. The Civil Rights Act of 1964 would have only been a year old. Mother and I were in a small restaurant in Texas with my grandmother when it became clear that MamaMay was uncomfortable that there were black customers present. I can't remember, but if I tried to say anything, I'm sure Mother would have shushed me and tried to draw my grandmother's attention to something else. Later, in an attempt to explain my grandmother's obvious prejudice, my mother mentioned that my great-grandmother Jane had taught my grandmother to cover her nose with a handkerchief when she passed a black person. Startled and embarrassed by this explanation, I asked, "Why?" Mother responded with something like "because of the smell." I was embarrassed to learn that my grandmother thought black people smelled.

Nineteen
Texas Land

I went to visit my aunt and uncle in Texas in the summer of 2007. This time, on our regular trip to Files Valley, I paid special attention to the creek. I snapped pictures at a spot where the road crossed over the creek. When I expressed more interest in the creek, Oscar Lee turned onto a dirt road, drove down onto a concrete pad in the middle of the creek that formed a low-water crossing, and stopped his big red truck. I got out. Though it was a hot August day, the temperature was a good bit cooler in the shade beside the stream. I sat down on a small flat rock next to the water, took off my shoes and socks, and plunged my feet into the stream. The shallow water was cool and clear as I settled my feet on the mud and stones a few inches below the surface.

It was not quite the same as when I had been there with my grandmother, what with the concrete pad right beside me and the shining new truck looming above. But it was the same creek bed I had played in as a child, the same banks with a tangle of bushes, roots, and trees. It was the same creek my grandmother had played in as a child and the same creek Jane Simpson had come to live beside in 1866 when she married F. M. Files.

In recent summers, I have often had an almost overwhelming urge to drive to the mountains of North Carolina and put my feet in a cool mountain stream. I thought it was because I love the shining trees and soft embrace of our Blue Ridge. But now I realize that it's this stream I long for and the shocking moment when tender skin meets water and the body experiences relief.

Sometimes on these outings to see to cows or to visit Files Valley, my uncle Oscar Lee would talk about the land around Grandview. He seemed to think they were fortunate to have three distinct kinds of soil in the area: loam, sand, and white rock. Loam, the rich black land that's good for farming, stretches from just south of Grandview all the way down past Waco and Austin.

The land north and west of Grandview is all sandy. It's post oak country, poor land for farming. Post oaks are short scrubby-looking trees with wood that's better for fence posts and barbecue fires than for lumber. My uncle called it "real cheap country." But land in that area sold for a lot of money in recent years, because when people from the cities want to move to the country, they don't like building houses on the bald prairie, so they pay more for a piece of property with some trees on it.

The third kind of soil in the region is white rock. My uncle always says, "white rock up on the mountain." There are no real mountains in that part of Texas. What he means is the slight rise in the ground next to the valley. The white rock has eroded more slowly than the land around it leaving a rise, or what folks call a mountain in an otherwise flat or gently rolling countryside. My uncle says you have to know about the soil and what's under it. For instance, if you build a pond in the white rock country, the water all runs out.

The land "up on the mountain" looks gravelly, and the grass it grows is scraggly. My uncle says the problem is that people broke all that land out to farm it and there wasn't enough topsoil on it. It should never have been plowed up in the first place, but our ancestors didn't know that 150 years ago. Today most of the white rock country is pastureland. People know not to try to farm it. What grass has come back turns out to be good for grazing, but you have to treat it very gently, according to my uncle. That white rock has lots of minerals in it and produces grass that is really good for the cattle.

This turned out to be a good area for my ancestors. The Files became prosperous farmers, ranchers, and cattlemen. The Simpsons fled to Texas with no idea that they would put down deep roots or that their children would be fruitful, multiply, and help to populate the state.

Twenty
Jane & Frank

After the war, Jane Simpson married Francis Marion Files, whom everyone called Frank, a Presbyterian with Old South roots like her own. The Files came to Texas more than twenty years before the Simpsons. Frank's father, David Sidney Files, brought his family to the state in 1837, just a year after the Texas Revolution (when Texas broke from Mexico and became its own country). David Sidney had been born in South Carolina, but his family moved to Georgia when he was still a boy. He married Sarah Ann Smith, in 1828, and had three sons before moving the family to Mississippi for a year and then to the Republic of Texas. For the rest of his life, Frank would recall crossing the Mississippi River as a small boy barely three years of age.

Once inside the new Republic of Texas, the Files settled first in Montgomery County, where they built a home near a canebrake inhabited by wolves and Indians. Their only farm tools were a broad ax, a garden hoe, and a sharpened stick, but they managed to plant a crop in rich soil and produce a good harvest the very first year. After living in the county for three years, David Sidney was granted 1,280 acres of land, which he worked for a time. The family moved twice more, once to Leon County and then to Grimes County, before moving north (in about 1850) to the "grand prairie" in what would become Hill County and Files Valley.

When my ancestors arrived in Files Valley, they found a beautiful wilderness with grass as high as a grown man and plenty of wild game. The Texas Rangers had cleared the area of Native Americans just a few years before to make way for white settlers. My ancestors found Indian structures still standing along the creek, scaffolds used for curing buffalo hides and roasting meat.

It is hard to hold the fact that the beautiful little creek I enjoyed so much as a child was stolen from Native Americans a hundred years before. The Indians living in the area had been forcefully removed or killed to make way for my family. Everywhere my people went in this country, they displaced native people who had been living on the land.

David Sidney Files built the first log house in the Files Valley area and floored one room of the house with rock. In 1874 he helped to establish the Files Valley Presbyterian Church. He brought the first herd of Texas Longhorn cattle to the area at a time when there were few cattle anywhere in Texas. He acquired hundreds of acres of land, established a farm on Files Creek, and developed a prosperous cattle ranching business in the surrounding countryside.

* * *

Frances Marion Files married Jane Simpson in 1866. He tells it this way.

> I came back from the war on furlough and my aunt Susan took me aside one day and said, "Frank I've got a girl for you. Her name is Jane Simpson and her family has just moved into Texas from Arkansas." I told her I belonged to the army then but I would meet her when I returned home. Sure enough I did meet her and we were married in '65 [sic]. I used to make her mad by telling her her family refugeed to Texas. You know in the old days some of the pioneers came to Texas because they couldn't stay in the United States. And it was pretty risky business to ask a man what he did before he moved to Texas. Her folks came to the new country to homestead as we had done, but I could always start an argument with her by referring to her as a "refugee."[58]

Frank and Jane actually got married in 1866. If Frank Files mixed up the year they got married, he wouldn't be the first person. That aside, he and Jane were married for fifty-nine years and produced ten children, nine of whom lived into adulthood. They raised the family in Files Valley, on 160 acres given to Frank by his father, in a house Frank built for Jane after they married. It was a "dog run" house, meaning that a dog could run through the open breezeway in the middle. The house seemed small for all those people—Frank, Jane, and nine children—but I remember my grandmother's reverence for the pretty little farmhouse even after it became vacant and the paint began to peel.

The house was surrounded by an iron fence and shaded by Chinaberry trees. My grandmother pointed them out whenever we visited her home place. The smallish trees had narrow pointed leaves and clusters of yellow berries that dry to hard white spheres in winter and cling to the branch for months after the leaves are gone. By 2005, the last time I remember walking on the property with my uncle Oscar Lee, the house was gone, having been moved a few miles away by some family member. But I broke off a branch of chinaberries and took it back to Durham.

A few months later, I was thrilled to find a chinaberry tree at the back entrance of a building that, for a time, housed *The Independent*, our weekly progressive newspaper in Durham. I was visiting a friend who worked for the newspaper when I noticed the tree next to the old red brick factory turned office building. Then a few years later, I was happy to find some of the trees at the Stone House, a retreat center thirty miles west of Durham. While strolling across an open field one bright winter day, I spotted the berries at the edge of the woods, shining like tiny lights in the winter landscape.

The pretty trees with lovely yellow fall foliage and bright berries turn out to be imports and rather unwelcome neighbors. Birds love the berries, eat them, and spread the seeds freely. The trees grow so well that they crowd out native trees and plants, earning them a reputation as invasives. In this way, they remind me of my ancestors and the many white people who moved west. First they (we) depleted the soil on the East Coast and then, after moving west, dug up the prairies in the middle of the country and turned them into a dust bowl. They wore out the land everywhere they settled and later sucked the natural resources out of the ground. My ancestors enslaved Africans and ran native people off their land first in the Carolinas and then in Texas. And these are the ancestors I claim to love. It's not easy or simple to hold these contradictions. We call them pioneers, but we might better refer to ourselves as the invaders or the conquering hordes.

***

About a year after they married, Frank and Jane had their first child. Baby Ambrose was born in Files Valley, on June 14, 1867, and died three months later. Losing a child is hard. It is one of the hardest things that can happen to a parent. Jane was still a newlywed, living in Files Valley among her husband's people, trying to hold her newest heartbreak. It seems particularly sad that she lost the child she had named for her brother who died during the war.

I was a little surprised to notice that Jane's second child, Martha Ann (Mattie), wasn't born in Files Valley, though that's where Frank and Jane lived for more than twenty years. Mattie was born in Blooming Grove in 1868. My best guess is that after losing her first child, Jane was nervous about the second baby. She must have traveled to be with female relatives for the birth of this child. Plus, there was the added attraction of a doctor in the Blooming Grove part of the family. Jane's older sister Sarah Simpson Davis and her husband Dr. Davis lived there, as did Jane's stepmother, Henrietta. Pearson and Henrietta had moved to Blooming Grove just before he died in January 1868. Later, after Jane had her second child, Henrietta married Dr. William D. Grady and stayed in Blooming Grove.

Giving birth can be a frightening experience for a woman, even today where expert medical care and midwifery are available. It would have been at least as unsettling an experience 150 years ago.

On October 30, 1862, Harriet Person Perry, pregnant with her second child, wrote to her husband about her fears.

> I feel very anxious and concerned about myself being here alone at this time. I cannot sleep at night—I experience daily & nightly all the horrors of giving birth to an infant in mind, & the recollection of it is as vivid as the hour of my baby's birth—I dread it much more, for I know how bad it is—my being alone is worst still.... Oh if you were with me, this trying time would be robbed of half its fears and terrors—I hope & pray you can come—but I shall try not to expect you for fear of being disappointed.[59]

Jane and her second baby must have gotten along fine, though we do not have details of the birth. We do know that baby Mattie eventually grew up, got married, had children of her own, and lived to be ninety-two years old.

CHISHOLM TRAIL

Another reason Jane might have gone over to Blooming Grove to have her second child was that her husband, Frank, might have been away on a cattle drive.

Frank Files built on his father's success as a cattleman. After the Civil War, Frank drove cattle from Texas to Kansas on the Chisholm Trail. That's right, just like in the movies. Recently when I stopped to wonder why anyone would do that, I discovered how the system developed.

A growing demand for beef back East after the war inspired clever businessmen to figure out how to get cattle from Texas to the Atlantic coast. Once the Kansas Pacific Railroad was persuaded to lay a track into the hamlet of Abilene, Kansas, and stockyards could be built there, the cheapest method of transport was to walk the cattle from Texas to the railhead in Kansas. A trail boss, ten cowboys, a cook, and a horse wrangler could trail 2,500 cattle in three months for sixty to seventy-five cents a head.[60]

The trail, which passed within a few miles of Files Valley, drew heavily from ranches south of San Antonio. It passed near Waco, Hillsboro, and Ft. Worth (which later became a Texas cow town when the railroad was built there in the mid-1870s.) It then headed northward, crossing the Red River at "Red River Station," then up through Duncan and Enid in what would later become Oklahoma, and up to Caldwell, Kansas, and then on to Abilene.

The cattle drives got to be quite a production. Herds averaged 2,500–3,000 head of cattle and were spaced about ten miles apart so that each herd could spend the night at a designated watering hole. And the amazing thing to me is that all that walking didn't seem to hurt the animals. Cattle that were allowed to mosey along at about ten miles per day and given plenty of time to eat and drink could actually gain weight on the 500-mile walk from Hill County to the railroad in Kansas.

The Chisholm Trail was used from 1867 until the early 1880s with the busiest years being 1871 and 1873. After 1881, ranges were fenced in what would become Oklahoma, and Kansas prohibited the entry of Texas cattle because of a Texas bovine fever. These actions, along with an 1887 blizzard, damaged much of the cattle industry. By the time of the Oklahoma Land Rush in 1889, which allowed settlement of much of the open lands, trailing cattle from Texas to Kansas was over.

Francis Marion Files became a wealthy Texas landowner and cattleman, eventually owning 9,000 acres of land and as many as 3,000 head of cattle at once. My relatives liked to say that when he rode a horse from Files Valley to the county seat in Hillsboro, about twenty miles away, he rode across his own land and then across the property of only one or two other men.

As time went on, the house Frank built for Jane got crowded. Nine of their children lived to adulthood, seven girls and two boys. It was a lot of people for a small farmhouse. My grandmother May, the youngest, shared a bed with some of her sisters, but when visitors arrived, everyone got rearranged. Some mornings, May would wake to find she had been put out of the bed and had slept the night on a pallet of quilts on the floor at the end of the bed. I found this story amusing, since as an only child, I had often had more room and more beds than I needed or wanted.

* * *

While my grandmother was still a child, her father's interests shifted from farming and ranching toward banking and running a cotton gin. As a result, Frank and Jane moved the family off the farm and into nearby Itasca. The house in town was large enough to accommodate the family gatherings when May's older siblings (six sisters and two brothers) came with their families. Frances Marion and Jane Simpson Files raised their nine handsome, intelligent children and sent them all to college.

Over the years, Frank Files built quite a successful career in land trading, banking, and other business ventures. A 1924 newspaper story about him reports that he acquired some land in West Texas and later sold it for $90,000 (a huge sum 100 years ago). The payment included one check for $50,000. The article says, "He carried [the check] to Waxahachie and put it on the cashier's desk at the bank there. The cashier looked at the check and turned to him and said: 'What do you want me to do, Frank, give you the bank?'" Frank said the cashier was relieved, "When I told him I wanted to deposit the check instead of cashing it."[61]

Most of his life, Frank Files was a lucky man, and most of his business ventures went well. He did invest in one disastrous venture—building a couple of compressors in nearby towns. But as the newspaper article says, he managed to pay off the debts and reestablish himself.

Frank lived to be ninety years old, and Jane lived to be ninety-seven. All of their nine surviving children married, and most produced grandchildren. One 1923 photo of Frank and Jane with their children and grandchildren posing on the front porch of their Itasca house has forty people in it. And that was before Mother's youngest brother was born. The Files filled up the Presbyterian Church in Itasca on Sundays and were a crush of people on Christmas Eve at Frank and Jane's.

Staring at all those Files relatives in the picture gives me another clue about why no one talked to me about the Simpsons. With so many Files nearby, that would have been plenty for my grandmother (and later my mother) to keep up with. Also, Jane's family was somewhat broken up. Moving, war, and disease took a toll on the Simpsons. Jane Simpson Files lost her mother in Arkansas, her brother Ambrose during the war, and her father soon after the war. She lived her adult life fifty miles from the nearest Simpsons, who were over in Blooming Grove. With no living parents of her own and so many Files relatives at hand, her attention may have shifted to what was in front of her. May was her youngest child, and by the time she was old enough to pay attention, her older siblings were starting to have children. She, like her mother, would have paid attention to the people who were in front of her, the ones who came to the Files family gatherings.

It was the same for my mother. As a quiet child and one of the youngest of Frank and Jane's two dozen grandchildren, Mother was a little overwhelmed by all the relatives who showed up for Files family gatherings.

Twenty-one
Christmas at Jane's
Itasca, Texas, 1920s

When my mother was a little girl, her family drove from Grandview to Itasca to attend the Christmas Eve service at their church, First Presbyterian. The little church quickly filled with Mother's relatives. She was among the youngest of Jane Simpson and Frank Files' two dozen grandchildren, and most of the families lived nearby or came to stay for several days around Christmas. A large tree was set up in the sanctuary, decorated with ornaments and paper chains the children had made. Gifts for the children also hung on the tree. When Santa arrived after the religious service, he distributed the gifts to the children, each receiving an apple, an orange, and a tangerine.

After church, Mother's older male cousins put the tree in the back of a truck, hauled it over to grandmother Jane Simpson Files' big white Victorian house a couple of blocks away, and set it up again. The next morning the children went up into the attic to get Christmas ornaments and decorated the tree, while wonderful smells wafted from the kitchen. The women set the tables while the men discussed the state of the world. Mother remembers her grandmother sitting quietly in a chair, watching. Jane Simpson, by then widowed and in her eighties, never raised her voice to give an instruction or to correct a child.

Christmas dinner could include as many as twenty adults and twenty children. Mother's cousin Mary Frances Cunningham Yancey recalls that the adults and older children sat in the large dining room, while the younger children gathered around folding tables in a room nearby, and the youngest ones were relegated to highchairs in the kitchen.[62]

This happy scene is marred for me by knowing that the feast was prepared on Christmas Day by the African American women who worked for the white families, including whoever was working for my mother's family at the time. This tradition of the family cooks making dinner on Christmas Day continued into my own childhood visits to Grandview and Christmas at my grandmother's or an aunt's house.

If the black women made Christmas dinner for the white families, when did they have their own celebration? What did their children do on Christmas morning while their mothers and grandmothers worked?

May Files Wilkirson

(1887–1974)

Twenty-two

May & Cad
Grandview, Texas

My grandmother May, the youngest of Jane Simpson and Frances Marion Files' children, was a talented musician. She went first to Switzer Woman's College and Conservatory of Music in Itasca and then to St. Mary's in Dallas, where she graduated with a major in voice and a minor in music. She was active in the Presbyterian Church in Grandview, and her strong clear voice was the backbone of the choir.

May's wavy medium-brown hair framed an open face with a high forehead, deep-set eyes, and strong chin. People say she was beautiful when she was young. By the time I knew her, she was older and might have been described as a distinguished-looking woman.

Once out of college, May had many suitors. She settled on Cad Wilkirson of Grandview. The oldest son of a successful banker, Cad had finished Baylor University down the road in Waco and returned to Grandview to live over the bank his father owned and to work downstairs. (When the banks crashed, the family got along all right, because in addition to banking, the senior Mr. Wilkirson had invested in lumber, land, and mineral rights.) Cad was tall, quiet, soft spoken, with a warm face and a handsome, straight English nose. As the eldest of eight and the son of a community leader, he had developed a calm way of letting people know that he meant what he said and that they had better not cross him.

When he asked May to marry him, she thought he was exactly the sturdy, reliable, attractive Texan she wanted to raise a family with. Her sisters had all married bankers or doctors. This young banker seemed a good choice.

They wed in the spring of 1912. On April 7, they stood before God and family and made their vows. I imagine light streaming in through the stained-glass windows and Jane and F. M. File beaming as their youngest was married off to a responsible banker, never mind that he was a Baptist and from a town eight miles away. By the time I was singing Sunday hymns beside my grandmother, the old sanctuary had been torn down and replaced with a sturdy brick one, but the windows had been preserved and reinstalled in the new church.

May wore an elaborate dress in the style of Queen Victoria. The bodice and long wrapped skirt are adorned with lace, and a spray of orange blossom leaves and buds is held at the waist by a bow. Her fluffy floor-length veil is held in place by a generous band of flowers, leaves, and dangling buds. All this for a wedding in a small church in a tiny town! Her father was one of the largest landowners and most successful businessmen in the county, and a fancy wedding dress was one way to demonstrate a family's wealth.

Like most young couples of their day, May and Cad may have spent the first months of married life living with one set of parents or the other. Both sets of parents had big houses. Cad's work was in Grandview, so it may have been Papa's house, but that house was full of children. The Files house in Itasca (eight miles from Grandview) was large but also had other residents, including May's sister Willie, who was widowed in 1899, and possibly Willie's sons.

At any rate, the oldest Wilkirson and the youngest Files set out on their life together. Before long, they built a house on Fourth Street right next to Mr. Wilkirson, Cad's father.

GRANDVIEW FIRE
1920

(My grandparents had been married less than a decade when their town caught on fire. This is how I imagine the day might have gone.)

May stood on her front porch on a windy Sunday afternoon in March 1920, staring down at the man on the steps as though he were a deranged intruder. "My house is *not* going to burn down," she insisted. "Mrs. Wilkirson, the Davis house at the south end of town is burning, and if the wind shifts, we could lose the whole town," the man pled, as concerned about her safety as he was about everyone else in Grandview, their bustling little town.

A single blaze on a windy day had been known to wipe out many a Texas town. Built of wood, the homes and businesses were as ready to burn as neatly stacked piles of fatwood kindling. All it took was a lightning strike, a brush fire, or a faulty electrical wire and a wind, and hundreds of families could be as homeless as their ancestors who moved into this area fifty or sixty years before.

"We'll be back around if the wind shifts," one of the volunteer firemen insisted.

May shot the man a saccharine smile, as if to say, "I bet you will." She didn't have time for this foolishness. They were just trying to scare people. It was like the headlines in the newspaper. Why couldn't they write about the good things that were happening to people instead of death and destruction? It was 1920 and everything was fine. Her parents over in Itasca were in good health, her husband was enjoying the job in his father's bank in town, and the lumber business was booming, what with all the towns growing up around the oil boom in the western part of the state. She and Cad had lived in this house for almost seven years, and now Pat was three and a half. She wasn't going to let those men scare her. She had a few things to do before she woke Pat and got ready for evening church.

In any case, Cad would be back soon from helping his father count the cows. She knew that even on Sunday someone needed to ride out to the pastures to check on the cattle, just to be sure none of them had gotten stuck in a ditch or under a fence. Her father was a cattleman, and she had learned early that those animals could get themselves in the most unbelievable jams. Secretly she believed that Cad and his dad savored these Sunday rides together as their time alone.

May turned to walk back inside, wrapping her fingers around the handle of the screen door and pausing to glance down the length of her porch to the fine two-story house next door. Her husband had grown up in that house. Nothing was going to happen to these fine homes. Those men from the fire department were being alarmists. This was Texas. Her father and grandfather had come from the East, raised their families, and populated a county (at least that's the way it felt growing up the youngest of nine.) Good lord, if men could build automobiles, surely they could figure out how to handle a little house fire.

She waved to her mother-in-law next door, who was out on her porch with some of the firemen. Miss Searce, as everyone called her, was her husband's stepmother. A kind-spirited woman, Searce had come to Grandview from Tennessee to teach music to the Wilkirson children. After their mother died in 1909, she took on a much larger role in the family and eventually married Cad's father.

Since they shared a love of music, May and Searce had made an easy connection.

When your new father-in-law owns a lumberyard, it does not take much gumption to assume that you will have a nice wooden house of your own before long. Cad and Papa settled on the big lot right next to Papa's house on Fourth Street in Grandview. May had already picked out a house in Ft. Worth she wanted to copy and had made notes and sketches each time she had a chance to go into that city just thirty-five miles away.

Once her gracious new house was completed (and furniture purchased or acquired from family members), she and Cad moved in and set up housekeeping on their own. She didn't mind cooking, but she always thought housecleaning was a waste of time—it all just got dirty again. I feel sure she had help from the beginning. There were 350 African American people in Grandview by 1920, so I feel sure that in 1912 she had some help. At least someone who could do some of the cooking and most of the cleaning, and eventually a laundress as well. My grandmother preferred to plant and tend her rose garden, volunteer at the church, and spend time with her relatives rather than to cook or clean.

Three years after she and Cad married, May was pregnant, and Little Pat made his debut on September 19, 1916. May was twenty-nine years old. Since May's sister Jeanette and her husband Pat Hooks didn't have any children, they named baby Pat after his uncle. The spitting image of his father, Pat would always be May's favorite child.

So, on that windy day in March 1920, May thought to herself, "That's ridiculous. My house is not going to burn. They will have to hogtie me to get me out of here."

She went back in the house. Little Pat was napping, or at least she hoped he had slept through the commotion. She walked into the kitchen to see if Fannie Alcorn had finished cleaning up from Sunday dinner (what we would now call lunch.)

Fannie Alcorn cradled a large ceramic bowl of leftover beef brisket and was reaching to open the icebox door. May intercepted her, lifted the cheesecloth cover from the bowl and touched a chunk of beef. A warm bowl of food could squander precious ice. She nodded, and Fannie reached for the handle, opened the door, and placed the bowl inside.

May would turn thirty-three on her birthday the first of September that year.

"Mr. Wilkirson should be home soon," May said, because it was what she had been thinking.

"Yes, ma'am," Fannie replied.

Fannie came at 7:00 every morning and stayed until 7:00 in the evening. The small family would have been lost without her. She cooked and cleaned and watched Little Pat when May went out during the day. She got paid $3.00 a week and lived in a house in "Freetown" that was owned by Cad's father.

"There's a fire at the south end of town," May said.

"Yes, ma'am," Fannie replied as she stirred the contents of her snuffbox with the blunt end of a kitchen match.

"They say it could come this way, but I think that is ridiculous."

"No, ma'am. Wind's not blowing this way."

May turned and walked back into the main hall. She loved this house. It was large and airy like her mother's house in Itasca. The spring air moved through it easily, if there was even the slightest breeze.

Cad and his father saw the smoke on their way back into town. Cad quickly stopped by the house to tell May he was going to join the other firefighters. Nearly all the men in town were part of the volunteer fire department, and it took the strength of every last one of them to fight a blaze.

While she waited, May wondered how her mother had done it, run a house with a big family, first out in Files Valley on the farm and then in town. It must have been hard even with help from the older children. It was challenge enough to get the baby dressed, get to church and back, and have a decent Sunday dinner for two adults. People said Sunday was supposed to be a day of rest and gladness, but so far in her experience it was a day of haste and madness.

When the second knock came at the front door a couple of hours later, May thought, "Now what? I'm never going to get these letters finished." She opened the door and immediately could smell the smoke. The man said, "Mrs. Wilkirson, the wind has shifted and the fire is coming this way. The school/church is on fire and burning shingles are blowing all over town. You have to leave. We will do everything we can to protect your house, but everyone has to get out. You have five minutes to gather some things and get in that car and drive out of town."

"What?" she said, her brain too stunned to make meaning out of the man's ridiculous words. My house is not going to burn. That's not what happens in my family. People die, but our houses don't burn.

"Mrs. Wilkirson, we have orders from the sheriff to forcibly evict residents who don't cooperate. You know you want to get your little boy to safety. Grab a few things and get going."

"Have you seen Cad?" she asked.

"Yes, he and the other young men are down to the fire. We are just hoping the water holds up. Some fellas have come from Alvarado and Cleburne with their trucks to help. Now please...."

At that moment, Cad appeared on the sidewalk. A buddy was waiting in a truck in the street. "May, it's time. Now hurry," he said as he walked up the stairs to the porch. "The water has given out. I'm going to the bank to be sure everything is in the vault. Dad is on his way to the lumberyard. I'll be with the other boys. We'll be fine. You take Pat and the car to Itasca. We'll sort things out tomorrow."

He kissed her on the cheek and walked down the stairs.

"Fannie," she called as she walked into the front hall. "Fannie!"

Fannie came out of the kitchen, her apron stained with dinner grease and was dusted with flour from the yeast rolls she had made earlier in the day. "Yes, ma'am?"

"They say the town is going to burn, Fannie. What should we do?"

"I'll get you an old quilt and start putting the good silver in it. You wake up Little Pat and grab him some clothes. Would you drop me off home on your way out of town?

"My peoples will be in an uproar," Fannie said as she untied her apron and hung it on its hook behind the kitchen door. "Never wear a dirty apron upstairs," she remembered Mrs. Cad telling her when she first started working there. It was a fine house and she didn't want to see it go. And what of her own sturdy little place? Mr. O. L. sure knew how to build a house. It wasn't fancy, but it had a good roof and had kept her and Annie safe. "We'll be walking 'cross the desert tonight," she said almost under her breath.

"Do you want to go to Itasca with us? You could stay in the cabin at Mama's?"

"No, thank you. I'd better see to my peoples now. Let's just get you packed up and get out of here."

May started up the fine wooden staircase to get Pat. There was no time to admire the carefully polished banister. *Don't think about the future, just keep moving,* she said to herself as she walked into his room, the room Pat had lived in all his short life. *Surely his room will still be here tomorrow. They'll figure something out.*

She grabbed a blanket off the back of the rocker in which she rocked him to sleep many a night. Spreading the blanket on the floor, she opened the drawers of his chest. She gathered up a few shirts, pants, and diapers. She grabbed two diaper pins off the top of the chest and tossed them on to the pile. Gathering up the corners of the blanket, she tied them and walked to the top of the stairs.

"Fannie, can you get this bundle?"

"Yes, 'um."

Then she woke Pat and hoisted him onto her hip. He was bleary-eyed and disoriented. She never swooped him out of bed like this. She looked at herself in the mirror over his chest as she left the room. She was still wearing her favorite Sunday dress. Not the best for traveling, but it would have to do. She met Fannie at the top of the stairs.

"Will you take him? I'll be right down."

"Yes, 'um." Fannie was about May's age, and she was good in a crisis. There had been a grease fire in the kitchen a year before and Fannie knew right what to do. She sacrificed a blanket hanging on the line out back and smothered the fire quick as anything. May trusted her now without thinking.

May walked into her bedroom. "Think!" she said to herself. She grabbed her wedding picture off the dresser, her hairbrush, opened one drawer and got a corset and two pair of underwear. There would be clothes at her mother's. She opened the closet and grabbed one ordinary print dress off a hanger and her everyday shoes off the floor. She closed the door carefully. That was all she could carry.

Fannie had Pat in her arms and the bundle of his clothes by her feet. In the center of the front hall was a pale quilt with her silver place settings in the middle. May put the items she was holding on top of the pile and walked into the dining room. She grabbed the three-pronged candlesticks off the dining room table. That was it. That was all she had time for.

She put the candlesticks on top of the pile of silver.

"Mrs. Cad, you take him and let me tie that up and haul it out to the car. It gonna be heavy."

May held Little Pat on her hip and the small bundle of his clothes in one hand and went out the door. "Be sure to close the door," she said over her shoulder to Fannie. She opened the passenger door of the car and let Pat scramble onto the front seat. "We're going to see Mama Jane and the cousins in Itasca," she said as she threw the bundle into the back.

* * *

Fannie managed to shove the clanking bundle of silver into the backseat and crawled in after it. She had wrapped May's wedding picture in underwear before tying up corners together. She was already thinking about what she would gather up at her house, just a small bundle of clothing, because she and the others would probably have to walk out into the fields and spend the night. Wouldn't nothing in town be safe. They had had plenty of rain in the last month, so the fields would be safe. It was all them wood houses that wouldn't be.

May started the car and headed north on Fourth Street. She turned left, went two blocks, and then right onto the Main Street toward Freetown, on the other side of town from the fire. *Lucky for the coloreds*, she thought. *Give them a little more time to get away.*

She let Fannie out at the end of the street to Freetown. No point in getting in all that.

Fannie said, "Thanks, Mrs. You take care of Little Pat. I'll see you in a few days."

May could see women, children, and a man or two rushing in and out of houses down the street. The men would have all been helping at the fire, but some were back now.

She couldn't go south through town as she usually did when she was headed home to Itasca. She'd have to take those awful dirt roads east of town out to the valley and come into Itasca from that side. It would be a bumpy ride, but the ground seemed dry enough. She should have packed a snack. Well, she knew nearly everyone between here and there, so she'd stop for water if she needed to. She should be home in an hour or two. There was plenty of daylight. And if she needed to stop in the valley, that would also be an option.

"Grandmudder, Granmudder!" Pat chanted. He loved going to Itasca and getting into the hubbub. There were always other boys in and out of his grandparents' house. He didn't know the difference between first cousins and second cousins. Cousins were plentiful and all the same to him.

"That's right, we're going to see Grandmother. And we are going to go through the valley on the way, just for fun. We'll put our feet in the creek if we have time."

She looked at the watch pinned to her dress. "Drive," she said to herself. Don't think, just drive. The good Lord who made her would have to work out the rest of it now. She knew Cad was sensible and would try to stay out of harm's way. This baby was going to be screaming for a snack in a matter of moments. That was her next problem. She could stop at the old Simpson place for a cup of milk and be sure the Martins knew what was happening in town. It would only take about fifteen minutes to get there. It was just east of the city limits.

* * *

Later that day, both houses burned to the ground—May's house and the house next door where Cad grew up. Neither family ever rebuilt on those lots. May and Cad had two more children: my mother, Mary Jeanette, and Oscar Lee.

Years later, May's grown sons, Pat and Oscar Lee, each took one of the lots where the big houses had stood and built a home for their own growing families.

Twenty-three
My Grandmother's House

A few years ago, while standing at my kitchen sink in Durham washing lunch dishes on a hot July afternoon, I was overtaken by an image of my grandmother's house. My air conditioner was on the fritz, and the house was warmer than usual. An oscillating fan blew air around me while I worked, and the sound of the fan transported me to my grandmother MamaMay's house.

Each summer while I was in elementary school, my mother drove me from Tulsa, where we lived, to Grandview, Texas, where she grew up and my grandparents still lived. Mother packed me up with at least one craft project and left me at my grandmother's for several weeks while she went back to Tulsa to do whatever grown-ups did when the children were away.

I don't remember being uncomfortably hot back then, though I nearly faint when I visit Texas in summer now. My grandmother's house was never air-conditioned, except for a window unit in the guest room where I often slept; but a big attic fan pulled air through the house, and oscillating fans hummed away in several rooms. I hardly noticed the constant background noise of the fans in those days, but now the purring of an electric fan can send me right back to the comfort and safety of my grandmother's house.

* * *

After the Grandview fire in 1920, MamaMay took Little Pat and went to stay with her parents in Itasca. I'm sure my grandfather was busy rebuilding the town, but eventually May put her foot down and said, "We have to have a place to live." He and his father were in the lumber business, after all. Rebuilding their big house on Fourth Street would have taken too long, so Granddad put up a little two-bedroom bungalow a couple of blocks away on Third, the main north/south street through town.

The house sat on a corner lot with a line of pecan trees along both the streets. By the time I played in the shade provided by the trees, they must have been thirty years old. I now live with a backyard pecan tree that also was planted in the 1920s. It stands like a stately guardian shading our house and reminding me of summers in Texas.

My grandmother's house had a porch, which faced the state highway that ran south from Ft. Worth to Hillsboro and Waco. MamaMay and I liked to sit in the metal glider out on the porch and count the cars that went by. Sometimes we'd watch for out-of-state cars, the ones with license tags that did not say Texas. There weren't many.

* * *

My Texas indoctrination began early, before I was born. Mother got pregnant in September of 1950. When she and Daddy went to Grandview for Christmas that year, my grandfather (Cad Wilkirson) insisted on showing them the oil field in West Texas in which the family had an interest. He wanted her to see the fields of "Christmas trees," the valves and fittings that stand above producing wells and look vaguely like trees. So, Mother and Daddy got in their car and Granddad and MamaMay got in theirs and off they went to Snyder, Texas, a little town in Scurry County that had been completely overrun by the oil business. Mother recalls her father saying that the Wilkirson land had previously been a cotton field.

It would have taken five or six hours to get from Grandview to Snyder on state highways in 1950. Mother doesn't remember if they spent the night, but they did drive through Snyder to look at the oil fields of the SACROC unit, as the Scurry County field is called, before driving up to Wichita Falls, Texas, where they stayed one night on the way back to Tulsa.

Papa, my mother's paternal grandfather, built lumberyards across West Texas, supporting the oil boom as it spread. He'd open a yard with a local partner, and then later the local guy might buy

Papa out. When Papa's partner in Scurry County bought him out, a piece of land was part of the payment. That's how the family came to own land in a place where none of our relatives had ever lived. Though the actual land with the oil under it was inherited by one of my grandfather's brothers, Papa made sure that the mineral rights (claim on anything of value under the surface of the ground) were shared equally among his heirs. In this case, they all got a tiny percentage of the mineral rights in what turned out to be a huge reservoir of oil and gas.

The SACROC unit is one of the largest "unified" fields in the country. That means the wells in the area all draw from one underground source, so the royalties are distributed based on the share of the mineral rights a person owns instead of the ownership of a piece of land or the location of a particular well. This is all of interest to me, because both my mother and I have lived off SACROC income at various times: Mother for the couple of years after her divorce and I at times when my paying work didn't completely support me.

**

As soon as I was born in May 1951, MamaMay and her sister Jeanette got in a car and drove to Tulsa. Mother and I were still in the hospital, where new mothers usually stayed for five days. Mother recalls that my grandmother and great-aunt were at our house when a man called to say that my father's stolen golf clubs had been returned, placed discreetly out under the blue spruce in the front yard. (They had been stolen from his car at the hospital while mother was in labor.)

Jeanette Files was May's closest sister in age and in friendship. She and her banker husband, Pat Hooks, lived across the street from the Presbyterian Church in Itasca. Though she never had children, Aunt Net treated MamaMay's three and her Hooks nephews as if they were her own.

My first trip to Texas came in September of the year I was born. Mother and Daddy drove me to Grandview, where they left me for a few days while they went to Houston so my father could play golf with Bob Hope (a then-famous entertainer). Mother had breastfed me for three months and then started me on cow's milk, which made it easier to leave me with my grandparents.

I was baptized during that trip, while we were all in Grandview. The Presbyterian minister came from Itasca for a ceremony at my grandparents' house, as did my great-aunt Jeanette and Uncle Pat. Another baby, my cousin Lindy Hooks Bullock, was also baptized at the same time. (Lindy's grandmother Janie Files and my grandmother MamaMay were first cousins, but I wouldn't try to remember that if I were you.)

Among Presbyterians, home baptisms are still allowed today if approved by the session of a church and led by a minister and a church elder. When I asked my mother if my grandfather might have been the elder at my baptism, she reported that Granddad refused to serve as an elder while he owned the movie theater in nearby Cleburne. My grandparents observed the Sabbath and wouldn't let their children or grandchildren play cards or go to the picture show on Sundays. But since the theater had always been open on Sunday afternoons, Granddad continued the practice when he became the owner, which made him somewhat less pious than the ideal church leader. The elder present at my baptism was probably Uncle Pat Hooks.

* * *

When I was eighteen months old, we moved to Long Island, where my father served as an Air Force doctor. He was drafted during the Korean War, having been in medical training during World War II, when most of his cohort was in the service. After a year and a half, when it was time to move back to Oklahoma, MamaMay and Granddad came to New York, picked me up, and took me to Texas for a few weeks while my parents went to Europe. I have always felt that this extended period with my grandparents was one of the experiences that helped me develop a deep bond with them, especially with my grandmother.

After my small family returned to Tulsa, we settled into a pattern of making at least two trips to Grandview each year, one in the summer and one at Christmas. (This pattern accounts for the odd fact that I've never witnessed Texas bluebonnets blooming in the spring.)

Getting from Tulsa to Grandview in the summer heat was not a simple matter. The Chevrolet sedan my parents bought in 1954 when we returned from New York was not air-conditioned. (My father bought an air-conditioned car as soon as they were readily available, but that was several years later.) Mother and I made many summer trips with nothing but a warm breeze to cool us. It can't have been pleasant for her, though I don't remember suffering. Sometimes, in self-defense, she'd leave Tulsa as early as 5:00 a.m. to make the sticky six-hour drive before the heat of the day was overwhelming. On one particularly hot trip, she remembers passing an air-conditioned restaurant on the turnpike and refusing to stop for fear that if she went inside, she'd never come out again.

By my personal geography, we were not in Texas until we got all the way to Grandview, which is fifty miles south of Ft. Worth on the road to Waco and Austin. Everything between the Red River and the outskirts of Grandview was still Oklahoma as far as I was concerned. I had no attachment to rural America except for the fields and ranch land around Grandview. That gently rolling open country was Texas to me.

* * *

My grandmother's house in Grandview was a one-story bungalow with two bedrooms and one bath. The front porch was set into the front of the house, rather than being tacked on. The public rooms lined up on one side of the house with two bedrooms and a bath on the other. Before long, they added a sleeping porch on the back of the house to accommodate the three children. By the time I knew the house, the sleeping porch had been enclosed to make a big bedroom with a bath. My grandmother slept in the big bedroom, and my grandfather slept in what was then the middle bedroom. When Mother and I went to visit, we slept in the front bedroom, because it had the only window air-conditioner in the house. When my mother left me alone with my grandparents, my favorite thing was to sleep with my grandmother in her double bed.

The house was heated by a floor furnace under the tiny central hallway. A grate in the hall floor ushered warm air into the house. I loved that grate. We had nothing like it in any of our modern houses in Tulsa. Only my grandmother's house had one. When I stepped on the grate, I could feel the grid pattern on the bottom of my feet. At home in Tulsa, I liked to play shoe store and would hold Mother's butter slicer against the bottom of my foot as if it were the shoe store's measuring device. It fit nicely, being about as long as my child-size foot.

The furnace grate was painted dark brown or black. With all the doors closed, the hallway was completely dark and, in the winter with the heat on, was toasty warm. In the summer, it was just dark. That hallway felt like the heart of the house, or perhaps the lungs. Most of the time, it was not a destination, but a place people passed through. No one stopped there except my cousins and I, who would close the doors, sit down by the grate, and pretend to be in a cave of our own.

* * *

My grandfather owned a Chevrolet dealership and a lumberyard, and unlike the sales people and managers today, he dressed like a businessman—in long-sleeved cotton shirts, long pants, and a jacket, at least in the morning. I have often wondered how he survived the Texas heat dressed like that. Wearing even a seersucker suit would make me want to faint. I feel sure he knew to wear a cotton undershirt to help soak up the sweat; otherwise he would have perspired clear through the jacket.

My grandmother served a hot meal in the middle of the day, even in the summer heat. "Dinner" was at noon. That's just what people did. The only cold things on the table were glasses of iced tea, sweating into their coasters, and salad. Congealed salads and dollops of mayonnaise were miraculously persuaded to hold together long enough to be carried to the table.

My grandfather came home from the car dealership and sat at his end of the table with my grandmother at the other, near the kitchen. My uncles often appeared for dinner, even after they were married. Their wives were probably too smart to attempt such a production in the noonday heat. When my uncles were present, they sat directly across from me. Oscar Lee had his own special chair; he liked the one with the worn-out springs.

A carefully pressed damask tablecloth always covered my grandmother's table at dinnertime. The cool smooth fabric fell in my lap and risked being mistaken for the napkin. No, my grandmother didn't do the ironing, Juanita did. In Tulsa, we didn't use tablecloths. My mother was a modern woman who set the table with placemats. It eliminated ironing.

When she wanted bread to be served, MamaMay would ring a small bell that sat on the table, and Inez would appear bearing a silver basket with rolls or biscuits she had just pulled out of the oven. My grandmother could cook, but she preferred for the hired help to do most of it. Sometimes she made me cinnamon toast under the oven broiler—white bread topped with bubbling mounds of butter, cinnamon, and brown sugar. And she liked to bake at Christmas time, but she wasn't very interested in cooking every day. That's why she had Inez. I can almost smell Inez's rolls and feel the dusty texture of the first bite of one of her flaky biscuits.

An electric fan pointed at my grandfather while he ate his hot meal and would have been turned to aim into the living room, where he liked to stretch out on the sofa after dinner. The soft whoosh, whoosh of an oscillating fan can take me right back to those warm summer days when my grandfather napped in the front room and the sound of women's voices could be heard through the kitchen door.

* * *

Life in Grandview was nothing like life in the modern city of Tulsa. Grandview only had about a thousand residents, and my grandmother seemed to know every last one of them. Our activities included going to the drugstore, which doubled as a toy store, going to the grocery store, and driving eight miles south to Itasca to visit my grandmother's aging sisters. She had six sisters to start with; five of them were still alive when I started school, and four of them lived in Itasca along with one sister-in-law.

The one I liked visiting the most was Jeanette—Aunt Net as we called her. Her house seemed fancy to me as a child. Aunt Net and Uncle Pat had built a nice one-story after their big wooden house burned. The new house had a large living room and a generous dining room; where I ate many lunches at her table with beautifully pressed linens, silver, and fancy china. (I now have some of her excessively fancy silver at my house.) My grandmother had nice table items, but her house was small; and after two rough boys and a girl grew up there, things were well used.

When we visited Aunt Net, I was allowed to explore the rooms of her house. I'd go in the living room and sit on each of the carefully plumped feather cushions on the upholstered furniture. The room was dark and always seemed cooler than the rest of the house, and I liked to listen to the cushions as they exhaled. Aunt Net had broken her hip in the early 1950s and spent much of that decade in her bedroom at the back of the house. As I remember it, life in her house was lived in the back, not the front, except for meals served in her formal dining room. She didn't use a bell like my grandmother; she had an electric buzzer in the floor near her right foot. When she pressed it, Naomi, the cook, would appear.

Sometimes my grandmother and I would ride out in the country to get corn from a real cornfield or peaches from a woman with a peach orchard. We'd eat the corn at dinnertime, but my grandmother liked to "put up" the peaches, making them into preserves. She'd do it "on halves," which meant she'd give the grower half the jars of preserves as payment for the fruit.

MamaMay cooked the peaches in the sun, like generations of women before her. She would put the peaches and plenty of sugar in big flat aluminum baking pans, cover them with cheesecloth secured by clothespins to keep the flies off, take the pans out to a small concrete patio behind the kitchen, and place them on a wooden table that had been the laundry table back in the days when the laundry was boiled in a big black pot set into a brick fire box out behind the garage. To protect the sweet brew from ants, my grandmother placed each table leg in a small tin can filled with water. The ants were smart, but not smart enough to swim these tiny moats.

The pans of peaches baked in the sun all day for three days and spent the nights on top of the deep freeze on the "back porch," the laundry and storage room that must have once been a porch. After three days, the cooked peaches were ready to be "put up" in jars. I never really understood the whole thing about boiling the jars and making the lids suck in. That was grown-up work. Watching the peaches cook in the sun was my job.

Peaches are a staple across the South, but when I looked into their origin, I found they are native to China. They migrated west to Persia along trade routes, found their way to Italy, and came to the Americas on the first explorer ships. Native Americans spread them across North America so effectively that by the time European botanists arrived, they thought peaches were native here. Peaches did so well in the American South that some feared they might take over.

> Peaches, not usually regarded as a weed, proliferated in the southeast with such fervor that by the eighteenth century farmers feared that the Carolinas would become "a wilderness of peach trees."[63]

On hot afternoons when there weren't elderly aunts to be visited or peaches to cook, I'd turn to the art projects my clever mother had packed up for me. There would be a ballerina picture to "paint by number," a small tray to decorate with tile mosaics, or cotton potholders to weave on a small red metal frame. The art projects made me just as happy as the peaches and the feather cushions.

A large mimosa tree spread its branches wide and shaded the side yard at MamaMay's. The tree was big enough and sturdy enough to climb, and since it forked close to the ground, it may have been the first tree I ever climbed. No one warned me against this particular adventure, perhaps because a thick carpet of St. Augustine grass below would have cushioned any fall. Fantasies were enacted and voyages taken aloft in those branches, a younger cousin or two along for the ride.

I watch for mimosa trees in midsummer as I drive around Durham. A long line of them blooms beside one of the parking lots at Duke University. On a recent summer afternoon, I was driving along a side street in downtown Durham when I spotted a lone mimosa tree. I pulled my car to the curb and jumped out just to bury my face in the silky pink blossoms and to breath in the clean, fresh, delicate scent that reminds me of freshly sliced cucumbers. That smell and the tickle of the fluffy blossom against my cheeks sent me back to a time when all was right in my world, to summer days at my grandmother's when presidents still rode in open motorcades, and my dad came home at night, a time when the world still seemed safe to a girl perched in a sweet-smelling tree.

Twenty-four
The Last Time

After my grandfather died in 1965 and my mother remarried in 1966, trips to Grandview became shorter and less frequent. I was spending five weeks at camp in Arkansas with my friend Sally Patton each summer, and Mother and I were staying in Tulsa for Christmas to be with my stepfather's family. Fortunately, my stepfather liked my grandmother, and his daughter was about the same age as one of my cousins, so we'd all go to Texas about once a year. When we'd arrive at MamaMay's, my stepfather would ask for a big glass of that "good Grandview water." He'd drink it down and go on and on about how much better it was than city water.

By the time I was in college and then graduate school, Texas became more of a stopover than a destination. I was interested in my own life, and my beloved MamaMay's mind was deteriorating. She died on June 1, 1974, when I was twenty-three years old. She had set me on the path that already had me headed to Duke Divinity School in the fall and eventually to becoming a Presbyterian minister. I didn't go to the funeral. I was in a prickly feminist young adult phase and a little uncomfortable around my conservative relatives. My grandmother had already given me her most precious legacy—possessiveness about land in Texas, devotion to family, and a sturdy attachment to the Presbyterian Church. Though my life would never look like hers, she had been successful in transferring her attachments to her eldest grandchild.

I come from a long line of Scots-Irish women—May Files Wilkirson, Jane Simpson File, Martha Simpson Simpson, the original Martha Simpson, and others before them. I now know more about them than just their names, but even before I knew something of their stories, MamaMay had made sure that I was never a guest but always a member of their household. Their claim on me was secure.

After MamaMay died, I continued to go to Texas from time to time for a family wedding or celebration and to visit Uncle Oscar Lee and Aunt Mary Anne. When I'd call and ask if I could come stay with them for a night or two, Oscar Lee would answer, "You bet!" as only a Texan can. He taught me to make the sign of "hook 'em horns" before I understood what it meant. I can still feel his large, rough hand holding my two middle fingers down while trying to get pinky and pointer to stand up. My uncle loved Texas and the land he worked as a rancher and continued my grandmother's work of weaving me into the family after she was gone.

The last time I was in my grandmother's house was in the summer of 2005, thirty years after she died. I was visiting my aunt and uncle. Mary Anne, the talkative one of the two, had had a stroke in 1999, but Oscar Lee answered all my questions in his slow, measured way. On the way back from an outing to check on the cows or survey my mother's land, we passed my grandmother's house on the main street of the tiny town. When I noticed that the front door was standing open, I asked if we could stop. Oscar Lee pulled his shiny red pickup truck onto the side street so I could jump out. I crossed the main street, stuck my head in the door, and called out. When no one answered, I went around back and found the owner in the midst of making repairs to his rental house. I asked if I could go inside.

The interior of the house was disheveled and the layout was a little different, but even with the changes to some of the rooms, it was still the same house, just sort of messed up, the way each successive owner can make a mistake and it adds up. But it was still my grandmother's house. I wandered through the living room, the bedrooms, and the tiny hallway. I opened the cabinet doors in the original bathroom. Those cabinets had always fascinated me. The house was trashed, but it didn't matter; the rooms were still the same shape they had been when my goddess lived there, when MamaMay lived there, when it was all of *Texas* to me.

The house was in such bad shape that if someone had given it to me, I'd have had it stripped down to the studs and started over.

It was really only a shell. But it was the right shell in the right location. My grandmother's stately pecan trees had gotten old and brittle, and only a few of them were left. But, along with her rose beds and the mimosa tree in the side yard, my grandmother's house lives on in my memory. It is the imaginative landscape of my childhood, and I visit whenever I am in need of solace or a sense of belonging.

POSTSCRIPT

My uncle Oscar Lee died in 2013, and Aunt Mary Anne moved to be closer to her daughter. With that, my last living connections to Grandview, Itasca, and Files Valley were gone. None of my closest relatives live there anymore.

Acknowledgements

It takes many friends and relations to write a book. Without them I'd be chasing my tail instead of *following a female line.*

Sally Thomas recognized Four Mile Creek in Mecklenburg County, North Carolina when I first mentioned it and led me to the trailhead of my research. Both Sally and to Amelia Stinson-Wesley, who live in Mecklenburg County, sent along local news articles they thought would interest me.

My beloved grandmother, MamaMay, wove me into generations of her family without my noticing and left me with deep attachments to her people, faith, and places.

My ninty-three year old is the last of her two-dozen Texas cousins. She can still recite their names, their spouses' names, and all of their children. Her connection to that enormous clan taught me to notice, remember, and value family connections. She has a better memory that I'll ever have and shared details every time I asked.

Melanine Morrison is an inspiration and steady companion on the journey to interrogate family connections, to better understand the ways white families of the South created, maintained, and benefited from our position in a racist society.

Ron Moss shared my enthusiasm, offered Moss family details, and turned out to be a distant cousin.

Dwight, my patient husband, went with me to the archives in Raleigh and to my ancestral lands in Texas. He listened when I went on an on about each discovery of a lost ancestor and when I rehearsed what I was learning about deeds, wars, oil, gas, and cattle--whether he was really interested or not.

His gentle support never e never let on if he was actually bored with thw whole project.

The groups of women that have assembled for weeks of quiet and writing at Trinity Center and who have patiently listened to various portions of this book, asked clarifying questions, and provided encouragement. Becky Wall and Maggie McFadden skillfully history and family stories, assuring me I could do it.

Peggy Payne provided editorial guidance, Marcy Litle read many drafts, Kaudie McLean checked every word and comma, and the grammar triumvirate (Liz Dowling-Sendor, Emily Seelbinder, and Carolyn Currie Hall, who don't even know one another) stood just and email away, ready to untangle phrases and sentences on short notice. These brilliant women reminded me that finally, I'm the writer, and I get to decide.

Notes

[1] Most scholars agree that the Scots and the Irish started out as the same people, possibly as a tribe called the Scotia in Ireland. As for the genetic homogeneity of the Scots, Irish, see: Nicholas Wade, "English, Irish, Scots: They're All One, Genes Suggest," *The New York Times*, March 5, 2007. If you want to get into arguing about how the Scots, Irish, and English might be related genetically, you can look at two books quoted in the article: Stephen Oppenheimer, *The Origins of the British: A Genetic Detective Story* (New York: Carroll & Graf, 2006), and Bryan Sykes, *Saxons, Vikings and Celts: The Genetic Roots of Britain and Ireland* (New York: W. W. Norton, 2007).

[2] Grace Cunningham Perkins and May Files Wilkirson, *The History of the Files Family* (privately published, 1959).

[3] Alister McReynolds, "The Rev William Martin: 1772—five ships and 467 families," *Ulster-Scot* (March 2008). Accessed http://www.scotchirish.net/forum/index.php?showtopic=4146.

[4] Daniel W. Patterson, "Backcountry Legends of a Minister's Death," *Southern Spaces* (October 31, 2012). Accessed www.southernspaces.org/2012/backcountry-legends-ministers-death.

[5] One interesting note about Rev. Richardson is that he persuaded his brother-in-law and his family to come to the colony, one of whom was an eight-year-old boy named William Richardson Davie. Davie was later involved in the drafting of the US Constitution, founder of the University of North Carolina, and governor of the state of North Carolina. Unfortunately, his contribution to the Constitution was the three-fifths rule (which made African Americans equal to three-fifths of a person for purposes of taxation and representation).

[6] R. J. Dickson, *Ulster Emigration to Colonial America: 1718–1775* (Belfast: Ulster Historical Foundation, 2010), 253.

[7] Partick Melvin, "Captain Florence O'Sullivan and the Origins of Carolina." *The South Carolina Historical Magazine* 76, no. 4 (October 1975): 235–249. Accessed http://www.jstor.org/discover/10.2307/27567338?uid=3739776&uid=2&uid=4&uid=3739256&sid=21102682251893.

[8] Suzannah Smith Miles, *Writings of the Islands: Sullivan's Island and Isle of Palms* (Charleston, SC: History Press, 2004), 34. Also *The Statutes at Large of South Carolina, Edited under Authority of the Legislature by Thomas Cooper, Containing the Acts from 1682 to 1716* (Columbia, SC: A. S. Johnston, 1837), 643.

[9] Jean Stephenson, *Scotch-Irish Migration to South Carolina, 1772: Reverend William Martin and His Five Shiploads of Settlers* (Strasburg, VA: Shenandoah Publishing House, 1970), 30–31.

[10] Janie Revill, *A Compilation of the Original Lists of the Protestant Immigrants to South Carolina, 1763–1773* (Columbia, SC: The State Company, 1939). When these Protestants arrived in the colony, the Charleston Council gave land grants upon petition and presentation of a certificate proving that they were Protestant.

[11] "The Journal of Alexander Chesney, a South Carolina Loyalist in the Revolution and After," *The Ohio State University Bulletin* 26, no. 4 (1921), 3. Accessed http://archive.org/stream/journalofalexand00ches/journalofalexand00ches_djvu.txt.

[12] For one version of Scots-Irish history, see James Webb, *Born Fighting: How the Scots-Irish Shaped America* (New York: Broadway Books, 2004).

[13] Stephenson, *Scotch-Irish Migration*, 91. William Simpson's land grant of 200 acres: "William Simpson 200 (b) PF 1721; 11 Dec 1772; in Craven Co., on waters of Little River, bd'd Jacob Jones, Elizabeth Caldwell, vacant land; sur. 9 Feb. 1773. (c) Fairfield, Laurens, Newberry."

[14] "Journal of Alexander Chesney," 3.

[15] The western part of Mecklenburg County and most of the Simpson land fell within the borders of Union County once it was created in 1842.

[16] John Files deed, 1766, Granville, South Carolina. 150 acres. (Copy is in possession of the author.) Sometime between 1765 and 1773, John and Catherine Files and their young family moved from Granville to Pendleton District, South Carolina, where the younger children were born.

[17] Lyman Chalkley, *Chronicles of the Scotch-Irish Settlement in Virginia: Extracted from the Original Court Records of Augusta County 1745–1800* (Baltimore: Genealogical Publishing Co., Inc., 1974), 303.

[18] Ibid., 510.

[19] George Washington and Paul Royster, editor, "The Journal of Major George Washington (1754)," *Electronic Texts in American Studies*, Paper 33. Accessed http://digitalcommons.unl.edu/etas/33.

[20] Ibid., 36.

[21] Webb, *Born Fighting*, 167. Webb is quoting from and footnotes Wilma Dykeman, *With Fire and Sword: The Battle of Kings Mountain, 1780* (Washington, DC: National Park Service, 1978). Dykeman is quoting from "Battle of King's Mountain" by Isaac Shelby, a pamphlet "to the public," published in April 1823, and reprinted in Lyman C. Draper, *King's Mountain and Its Heroes: History of the Battle of King's Mountain, October 7th, 1780, and the Events Which Led to It* (Cincinnati, 1881), 560–573. Pamphlet can be accessed http://archive.org/stream/cu31924032752846/cu31924032752846_djvu.txt.

[22] Webb, *Born Fighting*, 169.

[23] David Hume, "The American War of Independence," a lecture. Accessed https://www.youtube.com/watch?v=Q4HEY25acvI.

[24] Richard Maschal, "A Creek Runs Through Us: The Streams That Cross Mecklenburg Have Shaped Growth, Commerce, Even Life," *The Charlotte Observer*, May 6, 2007, page 1A. "Creeks gathered rural people into communities, gave their names to churches of whatever denomination: Presbyterians on Mallard Creek and Steele Creek, Baptists on Clear Creek and Reedy Creek. Such names created a geography of the mind. 'Steele Creek' or 'Long Creek' was how Mecklenburgers identified themselves before they used 'Exit 25' and 'SouthPark.'"
"Creeks also provided power. Farmers built gristmills and sawmills beside the running streams, grinding grain and cutting wood for themselves and their neighbors. The 1810 Census counted 21 gristmills. Creeks gave Scots-Irish settlers the means to express their enterprising spirit, an entrepreneurial bent that would flower in railroads & cotton mills."

[25] Donald P. McNeilly, *The Old South Frontier: Cotton Plantations and the Formation of Arkansas Society* (Fayetteville: University of Arkansas Press, 2000), 57.

[26] Easter fell on March 27 in 1853.

[27] McNeilly, *Old South Frontier*, 41.

[28] "The Ride South," by Jeri Rowe, *Our State Magazine*. Accessed http://www.ourstate.com/great-wagon-road/.

[29] Conevery Bolton Valencius, *The Health of the Country: How American Settlers Understood Themselves and Their Land* (New York: Basic Books, 2002), 20.

[30] McNeilly, *Old South Frontier*, 59, and Valencius, *Health*, 27.

[31] "Jefferson County," *Encyclopedia of Arkansas History and Culture*. Accessed http://www.encyclopediaofarkansas.net/encyclopedia/entry-detail.aspx?search=1&entryID=779.

[32] Valencius, *Health*, 42.

[33] McNeilly, *Old South Frontier*, 62. The settler's name was Trulock.

[34] "Immigration," *Encyclopedia of Arkansas History and Culture*. Accessed http://www.encyclopediaofarkansas.net/encyclopedia/entry-detail. aspx?entryID=5034.

[35] McNeilly, *Old South Frontier*, 60.

[36] Ibid., 100.

[37] Ibid., 129.

[38] Ibid., 101.

[39] US Census Bureau, "1860 US Federal Census—Slave Schedules." Accessed http://search.ancestry.com/search/db.aspx?dbid=7668 by searching for "Person Simpson."

[40] Henry Lewis Gates in "The Cotton Economy and Slavery" episode of *The African Americans: Many Rivers to Cross, with Henry Lewis Gates* (PBS series). In "What was the 2nd Middle Passage," on the website The Root, Gates notes that historian Walter Johnson tells us in his book *Soul by Soul: Life Inside the Antebellum Slave Market*, "In the seven decades between the ratification of the Constitution [in 1787] and the Civil War [1861] approximately one million enslaved people were relocated from the upper South to the lower South ... two thirds of these through ... the domestic slave trade." Gates points out that this means, "two and a half times more African Americans were directly affected by the second Middle Passage than the first one." Accessed http://www.theroot.com/articles/history/2013/01/2nd_middle_passage_slaves_werent_just_forced_across_the_atlantic.html.

[41] Valencius, *Health*, 27.

[42] Ibid., 27.

[43] M. Jane Johansson, ed., *Widows by the Thousand: The Civil War Letters of Theophilus and Harriet Perry, 1862–1864* (Fayetteville: University of Arkansas Press, 2000).

[44] Drew Gilpin Faust, *Mothers of Invention: Women of the Slaveholding South in the American Civil War* (Chapel Hill: University of North Carolina Press, 1996), xiv–xix.

[45] W. W. Heartsill, *Fourteen Hundred and 91 Days, in the Confederate Army: Or Camp Life; Day by Day, of the W. P. Lane Rangers. From April 19th 1861, to May 20th 1865* (CreateSpace Independent Publishing Platform, 2013), 84.

[46] Harriet Person Perry to Sallie M. Person, February 18th, 1863, Johansson, *Widows*, 99.

[47] Grif Stockley, *Ruled by Race: Black/White Relations in Arkansas from*

Slavery to the Present (Fayetteville: University of Arkansas Press, 2008), 50. Also, Faust, *Mothers*, 33. One Confederate general estimated that nearly 150,000 enslaved people were transferred to Texas during the war.

[48] Joel H. Silbey, *Storm over Texas: Annexation Controversy and the Road to Civil War* (New York: Oxford University Press, 2005), xi, xviii–xix.

[49] National Park Service, The Battle of Prairie Grove: Civilian Recollections of the Civil War, "The Recollections of Julia West Pyeatt." Accessed http://www.nps.gov/nr/twhp/wwwlps/lessons/70prairie/70facts1.htm.

[50] "Civil War Casualties," Civil War Trust. Accessed http://www.civilwar.org/education/civil-war-casualties.html. "Most casualties and deaths in the Civil War were the result of non-combat-related disease. For every three soldiers killed in battle, five more died of disease."

[51] Charles David Grear, *Why Texans Fought in the Civil War* (College Station: Texas A&M University Press, 2010), 109.

[52] Wilber Shaw, Jr., "Sketch of Frank M. Files," *Itasca Item*, 1949. Originally published in *Dallas Times Herald*, April 19, 1924.

[53] Theophilus Perry to Thomas A. Person, December 23, 1863, Johansson, *Widows*, 189.

[54] Theophilus Perry to Harriet Person Perry, January 8, 1864, Johansson, *Widows*, 191.

[55] Faust, *Mothers of Invention*, 31.

[56] Ibid., 30.

[57] Harriet Person Perry to Sallie M. Person, Harrison Co. Texas, February 18, 1863, Johansson, *Widows*, 99.

[58] Shaw, "Sketch of Frank M. Files."

[59] Harriet Person Perry to Theophilus Perry, October 30, 1862, Johansson, *Widows*, 51.

[60] Chisholm Trail," *The Handbook of Texas*, Texas State Historical Association. Accessed https://www.tshaonline.org/handbook/online/articles/ayc02.

[61] Shaw, "Sketch of Frank M. Files."

[62] Perkins and Wilkirson, *Files Family*, 60.

[63] Charles C. Mann, *1491: New Revelations of the Americas before Columbus* (New York: Alfred A. Knopf, 2006), 314.